RISING TIDES

SWIMMING THE OCEANS SEVEN
CHALLENGE AND THE TIDES OF LIFE

MARIEL HAWLEY

Copyright © 2024, D.R. María Elvira Hawley Dávila
All rights reserved.

       Facebook: Mariel Hawley
       Instagram: @marielhawley
       LinkedIn: Mariel Hawley
       www.marielhawley.com
       All rights reserved.

Design & Illustrations by:
       I AM Creative Studio
       www.iamcreative.mx

First published: 2023
Original Title: Marea
Translation: Paola Cohen
Reviewed by: Lalo Pérez

RISING
TIDES

For Andrea and Lalo, with all my love.

RISING TIDES

"My life story is written with salt and wind. Sea stars and constellations have left their iridescent glow; the flow of the tides and the sunlight have left their mark on my skin.

The language is that of the ocean, both powerful and magical, as its many currents that have guided my voyage within its deep waters.

Words are not just written; they are heartfelt; they are the ocean's imprint upon my life."

Mexico City, March 2023

"It is warm and damp - I feel the burning sun on my body. Oh how I had missed this warm humidity!

It's as if my skin can breathe; with each step I feel it closer and I listen to the roaring sound at a distance. I can smell the briny air, the smell of musky earth, mixed with jasmine, palm and rosewood; it's the smell of the jungle!"

Iguazu, Brazil, March 2020.

CHAPTER 1
THE TIDE BEGINS TO TURN...

On March 12th, 2020, I traveled to Buenos Aires to try, during the following week, to swim across Rio de la Plata from Colonia, Uruguay, to Buenos Aires, Argentina. This stretch of Rio de la Plata flows into the Atlantic Ocean. This is the final segment found just before its waters merge into the Atlantic Ocean.

Upon my arrival in Buenos Aires airport, I got in touch with Lucas, a friend and fellow swimmer, who was helping me organize the swim. He told me that the weather had turned and was not optimal for me to swim during the upcoming weekend. He urged me to rest or explore the different tourist attractions so that I could postpone my swim to the following Monday or Tuesday. As I ended the call, I knew for certain the place I wanted to explore: Iguazu.

The following day, a Friday, we boarded a flight to Puerto Iguazu. We planned on visiting Iguazu National Park to explore the waterfalls and the surrounding area. We would return to Buenos Aires on Sunday evening to prepare for the swim the following day.

That Friday at Iguazu, we tried to buy tickets to visit the park on the Argentinian side for the following day. However, we discovered that the park would be closed on Saturday but would be open on the Brazilian side. We hired a taxi that offered to take us to the entrance of the park so that we would avoid the long lines that were common when traveling by bus at the border between Argentina and Brazil.

We would leave the hotel at dawn to get ahead of traffic and planned to arrive at the park early, just as it would open, so we could make the most of our visit.

When we arrived at the park, I recall that many people were already there. I heard someone mention that the park on the Argentinian side had been closed because of the "virus."…I remember thinking, what a strange comment! Of course, I had heard in the news that at the end of 2019, there was a virus in China and that at the beginning of 2020, there had been some cases in Milan and other European cities. But I found it very strange that the park had closed because of this reason; it didn't make any sense.

At the end of February 2020 in Mexico, some isolated cases had been reported, but in reality, it hadn't been confirmed if these cases were people who had a common flu or if they, in fact, had been plagued by the virus. During my first 24 hours in Buenos Aires, no one had mentioned the virus, so I didn't pay much attention to the comment I had heard about the park closure and went about discovering and enjoying a day at one of the most emblematic places on earth.

We began our hike, and I felt excitement, anxiety, and a sense of expectation. I was sweating because of the exertion but also because of the level of humidity. As we kept moving forward, it was as if my skin breathed: it inhaled air charged with humidity and exhaled drops of condensed water. Every step brought us closer as I heard the sound of water, and in an instant, I closed my eyes to fill myself with the smell of life, feeling the damp breeze on my face. With my eyes closed, I walked a few steps ahead, and when I opened my eyes, I had the most imposing and majestic waterfall that I had ever seen. Its grandeur didn't fit in my line of vision. Its humidity enveloped me, the smells impregnated every cell on my skin, and the roar and energy of the water moved me, allowing me a moment of presence and mindfulness. I felt a sense of peace and was hypnotized to the point of being unable to blink. I was surrounded by a rainbow of colors, creating a magical space. I lost any sense of time, not knowing how long I remained still at the place known as "The Devil's Throat."

I began to envision the path of the river, beginning at the equator and ending in the Atlantic Ocean, a distance encompassing thousands of kilometers. The force of its currents was overwhelming. I could see a curtain of steam rise and feel the water drop in my soul's depths. I could picture myself clearly swimming in these waters. My journey would begin at a place many kilometers down south where these same waters flow into Rio de la Plata, and I felt a sense of power, which I would need to be able to swim from Colonia to Buenos Aires, a total distance of 40 kilometers.

I was awakened from my reverie with a phone call. When I heard the message from the other line, I felt like I was the waterfall, falling into the abyss as the vapor created a complete confusion within my rational thought. The rainbow was gone; I could only see the viscosity of the steam around me. "The swim is canceled! Argentina has just closed its borders!"

"Where are you?" he said. "I am at the Garganta del Diablo on the Brazilian side," I shakily answered. With a deep breath on the other side, he responded with intensity, "Run, Mariel, the border is closing now! It is just a matter of time before an official quarantine mandate is issued. Run, Mariel, run!"

I couldn't breathe. I felt frozen and couldn't form rational thought. "Breathe, Mariel, and hurry across to Argentina!" At that moment, it became clear that the waterfall's energy would not be my motivator to swim, but it would give me the strength to return to my country.

I crossed the border between Brazil and Argentina with an overwhelming feeling of anxiety. I was stopped and questioned by the immigration officers in Argentina, who could not understand the purpose of my trip. "I came to Argentina to swim the Rio de la Plata," I tried to explain, "and I was here visiting the tourist site in Brazil. I came into the country 48 hours ago when there were no restrictions in place." But apparently, nothing made sense. Everything had changed in a matter of hours.

As I had never done before, I ran with a sense of urgency to return to the hotel in Argentina where I had slept the night before. From there, I made it to the airport, hoping to fly out of Puerto Iguazu back to Buenos Aires.

For the next 36 hours, I tried to find a way to return to Mexico. All flights had been canceled. My return flight didn't exist anymore, and all other similar flights were no longer available. The city streets were empty, with stores and restaurants all closed. There weren't any cars or buses on the main avenues, and you could breathe the sense of fear permeating all around you.

At the airport in Buenos Aires, everything was closed as well. Every restaurant and many airline counters had shut down, and the digital monitors were black, without any information. I waited in line among other travelers who, just like me, had been left stranded searching for a way to get back home. Questions were left unanswered, and everybody shared a sense of fear and despair. These long hours of waiting at the airport became the link between a life I had previously known and a new reality that was about to unfold, a world collapsing into fear and the feeling of uncertainty that was closing in on me and paralyzing me.

After waiting for what seemed an eternity, I was finally ticketed on a Latam flight from Buenos Aires to Santiago, Chile. Here, I would have a 2-hour layover before boarding my flight to Mexico City. My eyes were filled with tears of frustration as I was thinking, "Everything fell apart." I closed my eyes and pictured the waterfall in all its splendor; I could almost smell and hear it at a distance. Iguazu, a majestic place, will always be written in my memory as the turning point between what it was before and what it would become after the COVID-19 pandemic.

I knew that upon returning home, I would find a different world from the one I had left before embarking to Argentina. I closed my eyes and allowed my thoughts to travel to another time, almost to another life…

"I have been swimming for over 9 hours, and I am cold. My shoulders feel heavy, and I swallow water every time I turn my head to breathe. My throat hurts. My tongue feels swollen because of the salt, and I feel nauseous. My eyes sting, and even though I am wear goggles, sea water seeps through. I am a few minutes away from stopping to drink and hydrate, as I do every 30 minutes according to my schedule to keep on swimming.

As I swim, I try to quiet the mind. I think of the words that I always repeat when swimming: "Inhale, I have faith; exhale, I am at peace." It takes all my effort to swim efficiently keeping a steady pace and helping my body generate heat to avoid hypothermia. I don't know if I will be able to continue. "I've reached my limit!"

Excerpt of Días Azules

CHAPTER 2
THE ENGLISH CHANNEL

The English Channel separates France and Belgium from England. The narrowest stretch is 33 kilometers wide, traversing it in a straight line from Dover to Cap Gris Nez. The ability to cross this strait is of great significance to navigation, commerce, politics, and even sports. In 1886, Captain Mathew Web swam across the English Channel for the first time in history. Since then, an infinite number of people have tried the same feat.

In 1926, Gertrude Ederle was the first woman to cross this stretch of sea almost 100 years ago. It is widely known as the "Everest" of open-water swimming. The number of people who have successfully climbed Mount Everest by far outnumber swimmers who have tried their fate and successfully swim across the English Channel. Even less swimmers have done so as a means to support causes which help others. I am one of the few open water swimmers who has set out to swim the English Channel to support various causes. My end goal was to obtain sponsorship to provide free surgeries for low-income Mexican children who suffer cleft lip and palate conditions since their birth. At that moment, when I was reaching my physical limit, freezing and exhausted to the point of quiting and giving up my dream, I pushed myself through to keep swimming for another 30 minutes.

This is my story...

August 11th, 2011, began as a cloudy, rainy day. However, being with my family in Dover was all I needed to make it a memorable day. I arrived on August 3rd, and according to my original plan, I would use this time to train in the bay and acclimate my body to the cold weather in preparation for the subsequent swim.

I would train for a few hours in the morning and a little less than an hour at dusk. During these moments, I would reflect on the first time I swam the English Channel. It was in 2007, and it was a four-way relay crossing. It was the longest distance that had ever been swum in a relay by a team, and only by a team of swimmers from Australia. Our Sports City Mexico team was able to complete the relay in a record time of 42 hours and 11 minutes, attaining a Guinness World Record, which still remains undefeated and in good standing as of today!

During those days in Dover, I missed my children and my husband, Eduardo, until they finally arrived. One by one, they came together: Lalo, Andrea, Eduardo, my mother, and her sister - my Aunt Alejandra. In that first morning, they came along to watch my training session. They were astounded when they realized that, even though it was raining and it was very cold, I would get in the water and swim for at least an hour. While I went about my early morning training session, they patiently waited inside the café at Hotel Marina Dover. After my morning swim, I joined them for lunch and went with my mother, my aunt, and Andrea to buy cookies, tea, and other supplies that would be important on the actual day of my crossing. That evening, we had planned to meet for dinner, but at around 5:00 pm, upon arriving at the Hamblin's home where I was staying, I received an update from Nora Toledano, my swimming coach at the time. Nora confirmed that Mike Oram, captain of the boat that would escort my swim, had called to say that even though the weather conditions for next day were not optimal, we should give it a shot. Finally, after waiting nine long days in Dover, the wind, fog, tide, and rain would allow me to swim across the English Channel.

A few minutes later, Mike called again to confirm that my

swim would take place the following day. Upon receiving the news, I asked my children, Eduardo, my mother, and my aunt to join me at the Hamblin's house so that we could have an informative meeting. I wanted to go over all the details of what would happen during the next few hours, but I also wanted to thank each one of them for being unconditionally by my side during this adventure.

I thanked my children, Lalo and Andrea, and my husband Eduardo, for their support in this endeavor. For allowing me to take time to train. For understanding my being exhausted resulting from continuous strenuous exercising for so many days.

I also thanked my mother for understanding what this dream meant to me. My aunt Alejandra, always ready to come on these marine expeditions, also received my gratitude. Not to mention my technical team: Nora Toledano, for being my coach; Doctor Ariadna del Villar, who supported me during my entire preparation (she was vigilant of my health and made sure I was in optimal conditions for the swim); Gela Limonchi, my dear friend; and last but not least, Ana Zuñiga, my colleague from Grupo Martí, who joined this venture and gave me her fortitude and support above and beyond any work responsibility. I was very excited and said to them:

"Standing by the shore of Shakespeare Beach awaiting the signal from Captain Mike Oram before the start of the swim will be a victory in itself. Not everyone has this incredible opportunity. Many other swimmers who have ardently trained to do so were unable to make it to such a moment - maybe because their training did not prepare them sufficiently or because the weather conditions did not allow them to complete their plan. I will feel fortunate to be there standing above the waterline, waiting for the boat's horn indicating the start, running into the water, and begin to swim. Your love will keep me swimming."

That night, I couldn't fall asleep until I finally drifted into a restless slumber for a few hours before waking up at 4:30 am to the sound of my alarm.

There is something about daybreak where the minutes seem to pass by quickly. When the sun begins to rise, and the inky black sky dissipates, it is but a small fraction of time where a mere breath is long enough for the light to come shining through. The moments before daybreak are

still, silent, and tranquil. But as soon as the horizon is painted with colors, it only takes an instant for the first ray of sunlight to come through behind the mountains or beyond the valley. It marks the beginning of a new day. I have found myself at this moment many times during my life, and I wait expectantly with emotion as I count the seconds with the utmost certainty that with those first rays of light, my eyes will illuminate as I get my energy and warmth. And as I close my eyes, I feel a sense of gratitude as I hear the same word loud in my mind: "Thank you!"

And so, that was the beginning of August 12th in Dover, England. I awoke feeling special. I had only felt this kind of excitement a few moments in my life. I felt full of life, and as I looked at the first rays of sunlight, I was full of this magical energy that would remain within me for many more hours that day.

We had prepared everything the night before, including the first aid kit, the hydrating and energy supplies, the meals for the crew, passports for identification, and the blankets that would keep me warm after the swim. Everything was ready!

I had only slept for a few hours, but they were enough. I felt rested and energized. As I woke up, I immediately went to the window to see the daybreak and await the first rays of light to fill my line of vision. I was overcome with a sense of gratitude. I was incredibly thankful for life, for this new day, and what it would bring. I was grateful that I had made it to the final stretch of this project and for the sense of love that had filled my heart in every step of this adventure.

I filled up on a hearty breakfast of oatmeal, many buns with fresh butter, slathered with orange marmalade - my favorite. I savored the sweet and tart flavors of the orange, trying to commit these to memory for a later time. I knew it would be a long day, so I tried to stay in that small moment for as long as possible. Meanwhile, the crew came and went, getting everything ready before the car that would pick us up and take us to the marina arrived.

I tried to remain calm, avoiding the nervous energy and tension that was palpable around me. With the sweet notes of the marmalade still alive in my mouth, we arrived at the marina in Dover, where we would board the boat. In the midst of the excitement, I said goodbye to my mother on the dock with a quick kiss and said, "I promise to enjoy every second of this journey; Dad is with me in my heart, and I will think of him the entire time." I watched as tears filled her eyes and felt my eyes soften as I hugged her and said, "This isn't a time for sadness. Enjoy these moments as he would have. Thank you for your love and for being my mom!"

I hugged my kids with all my strength, committing their smell to memory and getting my fill of their love. As I held them in my arms, I said, "I have been blessed to have you by my side; you are my motivation. This swim is for you, Andrea, and you, Lalo; you are the fuel in my tank that keeps me going and makes me stronger." We held on for a few more seconds, and Andrea said, "Mom, I don't know how, but you better finish the swim!" It sounded more like an order than a good wish. Andrea, barely 10 years old, was urging me to finish to share the accomplishment. She was able to see beyond the moment, more so than me. She was already picturing my victory. Hours later, in the middle of the sea, I would remember her words from that morning. But in that moment, she threw her head back laughing, spreading her cheer and letting us all join in her humor.

Feeling happy and optimistic, I got on board. My husband

and the rest of the technical crew were already on board, along with the Captain, the judge, and two other crew members.

I didn't have any time to feel nervous or anxious, for a mere 10 minutes later, we left the bay behind and arrived at Shakespeare Beach. Usually, this is where most swims have their starting point. In just a few moments, I was ready, having applied sunblock even though it seemed unnecessary because it was overcast. I applied Vaseline to my armpits and neck as a precaution as well. The judge proceeded to ensure that we complied with the rules of the Channel Swimming and Piloting Federation. As soon as he checked that everything was in order, he instructed me to swim to the beach. Once on the beach above the water line, I was to wait for the signal from the boat to begin the actual swim. As I jumped in the water, I felt a chill through my entire body. The water was colder in this part, so I swam quickly and got out fast. I couldn't stop shivering!

As I felt the sand from Shakespeare Beach under my toes, and while I waited for the boat's horn, I looked up to the sky and said, "Thank you! Thank you because every moment in my life has led me up to this. Being here makes me extremely fortunate." And just as the first ray of sunlight announces daybreak, so will the horn mark the beginning of this great adventure. I was still shaking, but this time, it was from excitement!

All at once, images of my life came to the forefront of my mind: my children, Eduardo, my father, my sister Aline (who was unable to come with us on this trip), my nephews, and my mother. I also thought of friends who had been with me throughout this journey and those that the waters had brought to me in recent years. I thought of my childhood with my grandparents Alexis and Maria, with whom I had shared incredible moments traveling and while on vacation. Also, my grandfather, Austin, and my grandmother, Carmen. In short, so many moments that have brought me joy.

With all these images in my mind, as if they were telling a vivid story of love and affection, I lifted my arms enthusiastically when I heard the boat's horn and ran to the water's edge, ready to swim. As I took those first steps, I knelt to pick up a small pebble from this side of the Channel (England), with feelings of excitement about reaching the other side (France), where I would pick up another pebble as a special souvenir of my accomplishment. Feeling an overwhelming sense of emotion, feeling blessed and full of energy, I could sense the weight of the small stone inside my bathing suit as I began swimming.

I was flying through the water! I knew it wasn't the best idea to start swimming at such a fast pace; it was necessary to keep a steady rhythm. But I was ecstatic about swimming the English Channel, so excited to be there that the feelings beat out any logical reasoning. The water temperature was just around 16.1C (41F), which was to be expected, so I wasn't worried. My training had prepared me for these low temperatures. What was a shock to me, though, was the salt. I can't explain it, but the water was extremely salty, much more than any other sea I had already swum in. Each stroke left my mouth with an intense salty taste, and I remembered the common phrase in my native country of Mexico… "salt is the spice of life!"

As I breathed in and exhaled underwater, I left a wake of bubbles of all sizes behind me. Each bubble reminded me of memorable moments in my life. As I was breathing in, I thought, "I have faith," and while exhaling, I thought, "I am at peace." The repetition of these powerful affirmations helped me keep an efficient rhythm of swimming that kept my pace and helped my body keep its warmth.

As I swam forward, I thought of the email that I had gotten the day before. The Foundation Alfredo Harp Helu, A.C. had confirmed that they would again sponsor my swim financially matching the number of kilometers covered by my swim, just as they had done when I swam the Manhattan Island Marathon Swim and the English Channel relay in 2007. The proceeds donated by the Foundation would go towards surgeries for underprivileged children suffering from cleft lip and palate (CLP). As I read the email, I jumped with excitement. I was full of energy after receiving the news, knowing that my journey would result in the aid of others. I felt a sense of accomplishment knowing that my efforts would benefit those who are less fortunate. My desire has always been to share and give back to others, and to do it in this manner has been a godsend. To do something that one is passionate about and, at the same time, help transform someone else's life is truly a blessing.

I kept on swimming as I recalled the words of a mother in Clinica Brimex right after her baby had come out of surgery, "Thank you for this opportunity." With tears in my eyes and a lump in my throat, I gave her a hug and said, "Thank you! For allowing me the opportunity to go forward without drowning." She had no idea why I had uttered these words, and as she saw me smile, she smiled back.

Only those who have seen a young child smile know that magic exists. It only takes a smile to give strength to the weakest of hearts and cheer up the sad and lonely. Those who can smile are just like small children who live a fulfilled life. With these feelings and conviction, I continued swimming so that more little angels suffering from CLP could smile.

Children can imagine fantastic things from the most ordinary things. They smile at challenges because they see them as an obstacle to overcome. They can't grasp the concept of time and never tire of playing, always trying to make more time to play. They will always try and will always negotiate to spend more time playing, regardless of the amount of time they have already spent on fun and games.

As I looked at the horizon and realized the long distance to my destination, I decided to adopt that childlike attitude. That of happiness and enthusiasm in my long journey to the coastline on the other side of the Channel. Just as children relish their playtime always making it a wonderful experience, so would I enjoy my swim across the English Channel as the adventure of a lifetime. I remember one day when my father said to me, "The way to become a happy adult is to continue being a child." And so today, I completely agree!

I was getting closer to the first shipping lane when I lifted my head out of the water and I saw out of the corner of my eye a set of large vessels sailing in front of me. These large vessels were lined up one after the other barely separated by a small stretch of water, sailing in a straight line. They were only a short distance up ahead. The second shipping lane is only a few kilometers off the French coast. In addition, there are many ferries crossing the English Channel, in the same direction where I was heading, that transport heavy cargo and passengers from Dover to Calais and vice versa.

Some of the ships that were there that day were carrying oil, others had large cargo, and some were tourist cruise liners. Regulations for any navigating craft in the lane stipulates that they cannot change direction nor can they decrease their speed. So this is what I meant when I explained to Lalo that maritime traffic would be one of many challenges to take into consideration when swimming across the English Channel. I remembered his words when he said, "Mom, you can do it!"

I felt a sense of tension when I thought about crossing the first shipping lane. I could see the vessels getting closer, and when I put my head underwater, I could hear the engines getting louder as they came near. When I was about 200 meters from crossing the first navigation lane, I saw Mike Oram signaling me, asking me to stop. As I slowed down, I saw the difference in size between our team's boat and the larger ships that kept sailing in front of us and leaving huge wakes behind. It was as if our boat was an empty nutshell, so small next to the other ships. Suddenly, while I wondered why the crew had signaled me to slow down, but then I heard a loud voice instructing me to swim as fast as I could without stopping until they notified me to resume my pace again. I quickly drank my carbohydrate and protein supplement, swallowing down my nervousness, and remembering Lalo's words, I yelled back, "I'm ready!"

The Coast Guard from the port is responsible for informing

all navigating ships that a swimmer is crossing the channel. We were short about 200 meters before crossing the navigation lane, and every ship that passed would sound their horn as a signal that they were aware that a swimmer was crossing the English Channel. That swimmer was me!

With Mike's signal, I swam faster. I could also see Nora and Gela coaching me to swim and move at a faster pace. I tried picturing myself navigating around the world as if I were one of those cargo ships crossing the ocean, but the wind picked up speed, making the undercurrent stronger, and I found it difficult to swim.

I tried to swim against the waves, but this forced me to use much more energy to kick so that I could swim faster. It was difficult to keep my balance using my arms to stabilize myself in the water. It took all my concentration and focus to keep up a much faster pace. I was also worried about getting too cold as well as the constant threat of the passing ships. Even swimming at this faster pace, I was getting cold!

As I felt the cold water around me, a conversation that I had with my daughter, Andrea, came to mind. I told her about the cold temperatures I had felt during my training sessions, and she asked me to tell her more about it. I told her that I had to come up with a coping mechanism to overcome the cold. I had started opening and closing my hands because I could pretend to scare the cold away. "What do you mean to scare the cold away?" Andrea asked. "Really," I said, "the hands are the body's thermostat. If your hands get cold, your entire body gets cold, and if your hands are warm, your body feels warm." She couldn't believe that it was that simple. "But that isn't all," I explained. "In order to really withstand the cold, you have to build your own protection shield." "Mom!" she said, "that sounds a little looney." "Not at all," I said. "If you eat the right foods, your body will generate body fat, giving you energy allowing you to move and generate body heat. So, it may sound crazy, but the body really creates its own shield to the elements." I continued by explaining that even in nature, this was true. I asked if she had ever seen a skinny seal. At that moment, Andrea started laughing. However, I said, "Whenever I feel the cold water temperatures, I put into practice the most important thing. Thinking of you and Lalo is the strongest motivation to overcome anything in the water. When I think of you both, I am filled with your love, happiness, and enthusiasm, and I have enough strength to move forward.

And with those thoughts, I am filled with warmth, and I can continue on my journey."

And so, with my secret powerful weapon, thinking about the love I have for my children, I kicked even harder, and I was able to cross the first shipping lane. When I lifted my head out of the water to breathe, I saw the largest cargo ship pass behind me, and underwater, I could hear its roaring engines. I felt the waves move around me, and I saw Mike, who made the "ok" sign with his other hand without letting go of the boat's steering wheel. My heart was beating fast, and I could feel the blood pumping. I knew my cheeks were red and hot, meaning I had made a great effort to swim fast. Crossing that first lane was as if I had swum 400 meters at full speed. As I moved on, my heart rate slowed, and I was able to regain some sense of calm. When I came closer to my guide boat, I read the message on the board: "Very Good. You crossed the first navigation lane." As I continued swimming, I worked to regain my rhythm and felt a sense of happiness and pride.

I was in the middle of the English Channel. I had been in the water for just under seven hours, and I started to feel hungry. So hungry that I could smell warm bread. It was torture! Onboard, they had been heating up bread to make sandwiches for the crew, and the smells wafted through the air while I kept on swimming. I couldn't stop thinking of sweet bread. That first bite of a warm, sweet bun always brings me back to childhood. My mind kept bringing back images and memories of delicious smells and tastes from my youth. I have always been a good eater, enjoying all kinds of delicious foods. Only on very few occasions have I lost my appetite, something that had happened to me during my previous days in Dover because of my acute anxiety during those days waiting for the swim to be confirmed. However, in those moments I understood that my feelings stemmed from the impossibility of being able to eat while my mind conjured all sorts of sensations from eating my favorite foods, especially the traditional Mexican sweet buns. I love the sugary combination of the dried fruit and the smell of orange blossoms, and I remembered how, at the beginning of that year, I had eaten an entire bun with the excuse that I had to gain weight to be ready for my upcoming swim of the English Channel. I also thought of that morning's serving of orange marmalade and how delicious it had tasted, along with the oatmeal and cranberry biscuits loaded with cinnamon and spices. But my favorite of all was the Mexican "gorditas", which translates as "chubbies", made of flour and filled with honey, butter, and cinnamon, and how they would taste warm right off the stovetop. All of these images were torturing me as I swam.

The crew had still not given me the signal to stop to have my feed, and I kept smelling their bread and lunch onboard. I tried to focus on my swim, but hunger was overtaking me. Finally, when I turned towards the boat, Nora signaled me to stop - I had been swimming for 7 hours!

It was around 5 in the afternoon. They tossed me my energy drink, which I swallowed quickly so that I would have enough time to eat something. As I had my feeding, I listened as Mike and Nora gave me the instructions for the next few hours. Weather conditions had turned. The winds had picked up, and I would need to swim against the current. I took a few bites of fruit puree, but my throat was so swollen that it became difficult to swallow. As soon as I took the first few bites, my hunger abated. This refueling and hydrating stop would have to tide me over until the next one.

The crew hurried me along. I would have to swim in parallel to the second navigation lane to make up for the distance since the current had taken me in a different direction. It was windy, and the skies were overcast. It was raining, a light drizzle that was almost imperceptible. I could see the crew's faces as they felt the chill. I tried not to focus on them for fear of getting caught up in the same discomfort. The light rain drops falling from the sky barely made any ripples as they hit the water's surface.

Despite the weather, I focused on the fact that it had only been a few hours ago when I said goodbye to my children and how I was heartset to swim the English Channel with joy and enthusiasm. I drew upon those feelings and continued swimming. I had to keep up those positive thoughts and hang on to those good feelings because, in the water, things were very different. My body was fighting the cold, which I was feeling exerting on my muscles. I had swallowed too much salt water that I feared getting sick and nauseous. I still had a long way to go, and the winds were getting stronger. However, I was certain that I was there because I had decided to do so.

I thought of my grandfather, Austin. He had crossed the English Channel, but not by choice. He was 19 years old, and instead of my excitement, he felt fear. It was 1916, and my grandfather had been part of the English cavalry that fought in WWI. He sailed these waters aboard an English Armada on his way to fighting a terrible war. With each mile traveled towards France, his fear increased. He was unable to control his seasickness and threw up during the voyage. Many years later, whenever he would recall those events, his eyes would get a lost, faraway look. Can anyone really overcome those memories of fear? Is it possible to be immune to the angst before battle or feel a sense of dread knowing you may be killed or have to face the enemy? In those moments, breathing is painful and hurts in the deepest part of our human condition. My grandfather Austin faced these emotions on his way to the trenches. As he looked on to France, his heart remained in England. With his friend Bramley by his side and his horse, Wish, his hope was set on returning alive to these same waters. What a different situation! If I was able to complete this swim, I would be victorious. My grandfather, however, didn't care about victory. He only wanted to come back home alive.

I kept on swimming, and I recalled that in its narrowest part (from Dover to Calais), the Channel measures 33 kilometers (20.6 miles). To me, this distance didn't seem so difficult to cross. However, there are many other factors that make this part of the swim particularly challenging. For one, the water's temperature is between 15ºC and 17ºC (59ºF and 63ºF) during the summer months. There is also the change in tides every six hours, which vary based on the direction of the wind, currents, and the navigating traffic. But for me, the biggest challenge was the water's temperature. So, I concentrated on keeping my body warm regardless of the factors that would determine the water's currents, if I could acclimate my body to the water temperatures, I knew I would reach my goal. How little did I know! At that moment, I focused my energy on my desire to swim the English Channel and everything I had done to prepare to achieve this goal.

I vividly remember the first time I confided in my father, telling him of my dream to cross the English Channel. He was overjoyed and offered to be my doctor aboard the escort boat. From that moment, his spot had been permanently reserved in all my escort boats. My father would be the first to climb aboard, and his spot was the first one guaranteed.

The next step came easily: it was sharing my dream with the rest of the family. They all saw the excitement on my face, and they supported the adventure. Of course, the training and preparation had been my responsibility, and as I swam, I realized how much I had trained to get to this moment. I had swum more than 1,000 kilometers (620 miles) as part of my training!

"It is commonly said that one must travel many kilometers to find peace. One must take a step forward and say I want to be at peace; I want to find my life and leave behind that which harms or saddens me."

Laguna de Alchichica, Puebla, April 2011

CHAPTER 3
WILL I BE ABLE TO KEEP GOING?

From the onset of the swim, there was little sunlight and a lot of wind. Mike Oram had said to me the day before, "We will begin with strong winds, but we expect them to die down as the day moves along." But as the hours went by, the wind became more intense and the waves became stronger. It was becoming more difficult to make any progress under these conditions. I was losing my stride, swallowing more water, and the strength of the waves kept literally tossing me around.

The escort boat was rolling so much that I could see the Mexican flag onboard nearly touching the water when the boat rolled on its side. I was wary of swimming too close to the boat since it could hurt me, as it had happened once before. However, whenever I moved too far away from the escort boat, the crew would signal me to come closer because they did not want to lose sight of me. The minutes seemed to pass by slowly. The crew still hadn't signaled me to stop. I could see that Nora, Gela, and Ariadna were worried. The wind carried their loud voices, but I was unable to hear what they were saying. I saw them hanging tightly on to anything so that they wouldn't be tossed overboard. I could tell they were cold, and they looked very worried. I was beginning to feel concerned as well.

How long could I keep this up? I had a feeling that I couldn't hang on to these conditions for much longer. I started counting my strokes: first to 500, then to 1000, until finally up to 2000, only to begin counting all over again. My shoulders were hurting badly. I kept saying to myself, "Come on, you can do it!" This time, I will count up to 1000 strokes. And so I would count them individually to ignore negative thoughts draining out my energy and my will. It was so unlike me. I never use these debilitating words and usually discard them when they have come up in my thoughts in the past. However, at that moment, I was reaching my physical limit. I could feel my heart rate picking up because of the cold water, the exhaustion, and, of course, the hunger. My eyes were stinging - even though I had goggles, some water had seeped through. My tongue was also swollen, and it felt like if it didn't fit inside my mouth. Finally, the crew signaled me to stop, and with tears in my eyes, I told them, "I can't go on anymore, I can't do it anymore!" As I let the words out, I started crying. I felt like quitting!

Nora threw me the bottle with my feed. I took it automatically without listening to what they were saying and, because it was warm, I held it with both hands, trying to warm myself up. I began drinking the energy mix, feeling some relief in my mouth. I was still unable to swallow because it was incredibly painful to do so. I thought of my kids and felt an overwhelming sadness that they would be waiting for me in Dover, full of expectations. I found the strength to drink and swallow the warm liquid until it was gone. I decided to continue for another half hour but to do so, I would need to eat something. I asked the team toss me some soup or some solid food. They threw me a small bag with mashed potatoes in it. I bit the bag open and ate the contents as fast as I possible could given that every second that passed was another second for me in freezing water. I could barely hold the bag with the potatoes. I was shivering! I was cold! Those few bites of food would have to give me enough energy to continue for at least another 30 minutes.

From where I was I couldn't even see the coast of France. My rational mind insisted that I should stop. The easiest thing would be to stop and climb aboard the boat. If I did that and decided to quit, I could get warm blankets and a hot drink on board. I could rest, and it would be the end of this torture and ill feeling. I never even thought I might give up, and that's what I was doing! I had just said it! However, my body automatically kept on swimming. And so I continued on my swim. But a few minutes later, the negative thoughts came back again, and I was shrouded in with doubt. Will I make it? What good will another 30 minutes do when I am so far out at sea? But I remembered the phrase: "Keep Calm and Carry On." And so I continued on. I gave myself half an hour to prove that I was capable of staying in the water that long. I kept going on and tried to stay warm and counter the effects of the cold temperature, focusing on the movement of my arms to not feel the pain on my shoulders. I told myself: "Unfortunately, these aren't the best conditions; there's too much wind, rain, cold weather, and it is getting dark. But I also realized that this was perhaps my one and only chance. It was only up to me to keep on swimming."

I had been 10 hours in the water. I knew this was my opportunity to swim the English Channel, but the situation grew more and more complicated as time went by. When the time came for me to stop for my next feeding, at exactly 10 hours, I would be dealing with two options: give up and board the boat, or continue swimming. This decision seemed easy -- but it definitely wasn't.

I carried on. Each stroke helped me move forward, and each meter got me closer to Calais. I cleared my mind and repeated my mantra: "Keep calm and carry on." I continued with the words that I had donned at the beginning: "I have faith and am at peace." I tried to breathe deeply. When inhaling, I would fill up my lungs, and when exhaling, I would blow the air out slowly, trying to center my body and bring it back to the steady rhythm that would allow me to continue for the next hours without succumbing to the pain or exhaustion. I wanted to reach a state where neither the waves nor the cold nor salt water would affect me. To do this, I recalled my daughter's words, "Mom, make sure you finish, huh?" I concentrated on listening to my breath underwater to feel the warm bubbles I was leaving behind as I exhaled. I visualized what Andrea had seen on the docks: her mother reaching for her dream, becoming a part of it, and sharing it. I was still far from the French coastline but I realized I could not stop. I would continue on!

As soon as I completed the 10 hours and heard the signal to stop swimming, I was greeted with encouragement from the team. The crew told me that I was doing well and that I should keep at it- I was getting closer. Their words helped me find my strength. I didn't want to get as cold as I did half an hour before - I couldn't allow myself to get hypothermic. For those reasons, even though my throat and tongue were sore, I gulped the warm liquid down. I finished the entire drink taking small but constant sips. I let go of the bottle and felt a splash in the water. I thought someone had fallen overboard. It was Gela, jumping into the water next to me! Mike explained that she would swim beside me for an hour before it got dark to help put the fluorescent light on the back of my swimsuit. This would be necessary for the crew to see me swim in the dark.

To think that only 30 minutes ago, I was ready to quit. It had taken all my effort to swim at a constant pace and generate as much warmth as possible to keep the cold at bay. Did I hear correctly that Gela would be swimming by my side for the next hour? Did the crew miss something? Were they not able to understand that I could no longer swim on for another hour? It was overwhelming to think that my body could withstand increasing winds, cold weather, and strong waves, along with the emotional and physical pain I was under. I would probably only swim for a few more minutes or so. An hour seemed way out of reach! My heart skipped a beat when I saw my friend next to me and we began swimming together.

As we swam, my mind brought me back to last October when it was my father's birthday, and I had given him a plane ticket to come with me to England. He was so excited that he would be accompanying me to swim the English Channel! He understood what it meant to take on this incredible challenge. He had been my medic onboard the escort boat when I swam the Manhattan Island Marathon Swim when I was a participant in the challenge around the island of Manhattan. During my preparation for that event, he was by my side throughout the entire process. Sharing that experience with my dad was one of the most inspiring moments of my life, and the idea of crossing the English Channel with him was a dream that motivated me to prepare even more.

What I am about to share next, is very painful to me; however, my story would not be complete if I do not add this narrative. So, it is necessary for me to include the following paragraphs here.

In early March 2011, as part of my training for the English Channel crossing, I decided to participate in the Valle de Bravo Triathlon. When I close my eyes, I remember those moments as if it had happened yesterday.

I was about to finish the cycling leg of the triathlon. I was breathing hard, my legs giving its all, focused on getting off the bike before entering the transition zone without falling of the bike in those last few meters. I was aware that the most difficult part for me was about to come and the most strenuous: the ten-kilometer run. My parents and my son Lalo came to mind, who promised to be waiting for me at the finish line.

Lalo and I were both going to do the triathlon. Normally, adults start very early in the morning and the children start at noon. So the night before, we had planned that they would arrive mid-morning to see me finish, and my parents and I would cheer Lalo on his triathlon.

As I pedaled the kilometers on my bike, I was looking forward to seeing my parents and Lalo in the spectators' zone. I also thought of Andrea, who had stayed behind in Mexico City with Eduardo so that she could participate in an all-girls soccer tournament. I could picture them enjoying the moment and having fun. As I reached the last few meters, I got off my bicycle and set off running. I had to make it to the designated area where I would change into my running shoes and begin the run portion of the triathlon. Suddenly, someone came to take the bicycle away from me, and at that moment I saw Lalo. I was overjoyed to see him. I was so happy that he was already there. As I got closer, I saw that he wasn't happy at all. He was very agitated and told me there had been an accident. My parents had fallen from a terrace, and they were at the hospital. I couldn't understand what he was saying. "My parents fell off from the terrace? When? From what terrace?"

Lalo took my hand and we ran together. I stopped and asked him with urgency: What's happening?" His face was drawn with pain and fear and I was completely confused. "Lalo, please tell me what is going on!" I begged. " Nolo and Grandma fell off from the terrace at the house we are staying. A terrible accident! They were taken to the hospital…I came to get you. The neighbor brought me on his boat. He is waiting on the docks for us so that he can take us to the hospital…" He said, crying: "Run, mom, run! Run!"

"Run, Mom, run!" his words kept sounding in my head. I took his hand again, and we ran across the transition zone of the race to get to the dock. Once there, we jumped into the waiting boat. The boat rushed us to the other side of the lake. I was trembling, feeling cold, scared, and I could hardly breathe, feeling like I was choking. I held on to my son until we made it to the other dock, where someone pulled me apart from Lalo to take me to the hospital. I ran as fast as I could. I felt the strain on my lungs from the effort, and I rushed into the emergency room. I saw my dad there lying on a gurney, and I ran to hug him. "Dad, I'm here! Dad, can you hear me?" I said. He didn't answer, so I hugged him harder until a doctor came to speak to me. I didn't hear what he was saying. I kept begging my dad not to leave me, telling him that I needed him and that he had to be at my next swim. The doctor kept trying to say something to me, but I couldn't understand what he was saying. He finally pulled me back and, looked me in the eye and said, "Your mother is alive." At that moment, my mom came in and reached out to hug me. Without thinking, I pushed her away. I only wanted to be with dad. And so when I was able to get closer, I saw a line of blood that was flowing from his ear to his neck, and when I reached for him again, I felt his cold body...this cold sensation broke my heart.

My mom reached out for me again. I broke free from her arms and threw myself to the ground. I remained there crying and screaming out of pain for a long time. I don't know how long I was there…one hour, maybe two, I don't know. All I remember is that the pain was too much to bear. I heard someone say, "Lalo is waiting for you outside," and I finally reacted and thought of my eleven-year-old son yelling at me, "Hurry, mom, hurry!" I tried to get up, but my legs faltered. I didn't have the strength to get up, I felt dizzy, and I had a terrible headache.

When I was able to get up, I saw my mom sitting by my dad's gurney, where he laid still. He was badly injured and still bleeding, and my mom was weeping as she held onto his hand. I came closer to her and hugged her. Little by little, I felt coming back to myself with that embrace. I was holding on to both of them, just as the day I was born. My mother had repeatedly recounted how they held on to me as I stretched my tiny arms toward them. At that moment, in the emergency room of the hospital, I felt my heart ripped open for my dad's passing and my mom's suffering and I stretched out my arms for the last time, holding them both together with my deepest pain and all of my love.

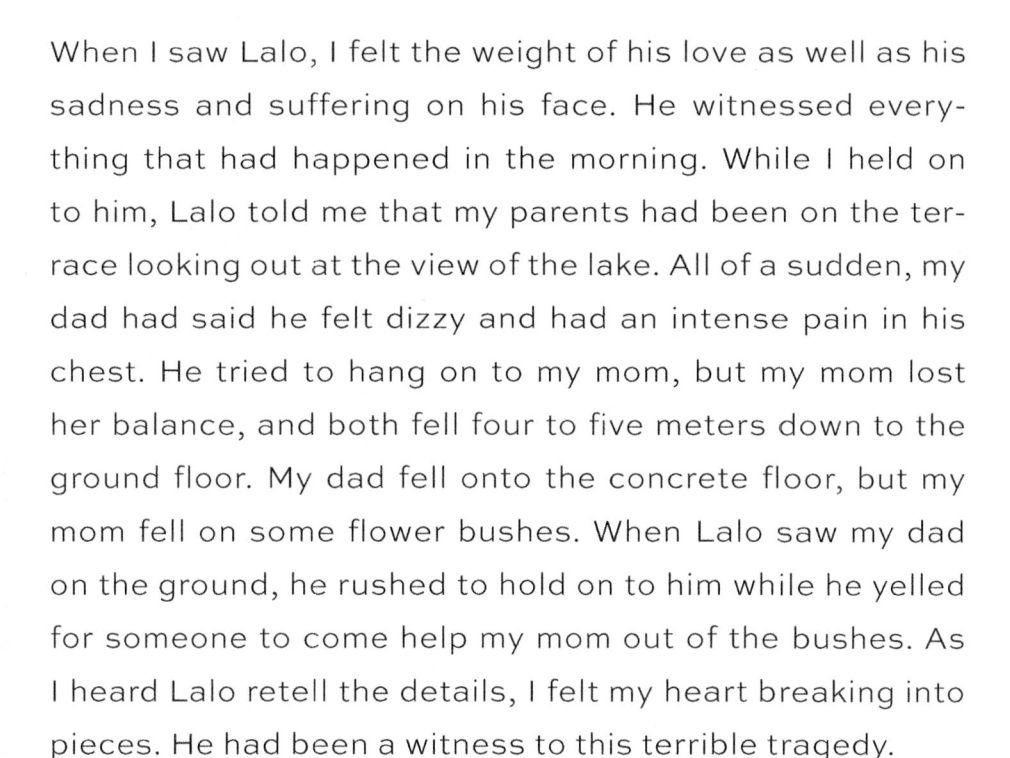

When I saw Lalo, I felt the weight of his love as well as his sadness and suffering on his face. He witnessed everything that had happened in the morning. While I held on to him, Lalo told me that my parents had been on the terrace looking out at the view of the lake. All of a sudden, my dad had said he felt dizzy and had an intense pain in his chest. He tried to hang on to my mom, but my mom lost her balance, and both fell four to five meters down to the ground floor. My dad fell onto the concrete floor, but my mom fell on some flower bushes. When Lalo saw my dad on the ground, he rushed to hold on to him while he yelled for someone to come help my mom out of the bushes. As I heard Lalo retell the details, I felt my heart breaking into pieces. He had been a witness to this terrible tragedy.

I hugged Lalo with all my strength, proud of how he had reacted at such a young age. We held on to each other as we cried, and I thought of Andrea. As soon as Eduardo heard the news, he decided it was best for Andrea to remain in Mexico City while he came to Valle de Bravo to help with the arrangements to bring my mom and dad back to the city.

Hours passed before we were able to bring back my dad's

body to Mexico City, and during every waiting moment, I relived a million scenes of my life when dad was alive.

When we finally got home, I ran from the car to hug Andrea. She had not yet received the details of what had happened that morning and she was anxious for me to explain what had occurred. I didn't know where to start. How can one explain these things to one's children? How does one tell a child that a loved one is gone? I remember the first time I went to Valle de Bravo when I was just a child, and I told this story to Lalo and Andrea.

My father's brother, my uncle Francis, had a house by the lake. One day, he invited us to spend the weekend there. My dad told me it was a beautiful place, next to a forest, but I had never gone to a place like that, so it was hard for me to imagine it. We left Mexico City around 8:00 pm, traveling on a dark, winding road. By the time we arrived, it was almost midnight. I recall getting out of the car, climbing many stairs, going to a house, and getting into bed. The next day, my dad woke my sister and me up and said, "Let's go for a walk; I want you to see the lake."

We began hiking, and I realized the house was in the middle

of a forest. It was wonderful. The pine trees almost reached the sky! We walked along a path next to many plants on our way down, and all of a sudden, I saw a blinding light. It was the water that was reflecting the sunrise on its surface. I stopped to admire the view as my heart skipped a beat. I remember yelling, "Dad, look how beautiful!" He answered, "It is very nice and peaceful."

Years later, it was at that exact same place where my father's heart gave out. My dad fell into a sense of eternal peace. My mom, over those bushes that softened her fall and saved her life. Andrea and Lalo held me as they cried. The three of us remember that wonderful man who had showered us with so much love during his lifetime.

How ironic that the weekend we had planned to be a special occasion for the whole family had resulted in one of the most painful moments that life brought us. The accident my parents lived through was terrible: he lost his life, and my mother would be forever scarred. When a death happens in such a dramatic way, it leaves desolation and pain in its wake - it leaves a mark that crushes one's heart.

During the days that followed, the world as I knew it had

completely changed. I faced overwhelming periods of pain, and I felt paralyzed with no way out. My eyes were bloodshot from crying, and my heart was in so much pain that I couldn't find a way to share my love with my children, who were also suffering. Lalo had witnessed the tragedy - he was the last person to see and talk to dad while he was still alive. The impact was too much to bear for such a young child who adored his grandfather who had set out to enjoy a weekend full of adventures in Valle de Bravo alongside his childhood hero. I could see him suffering over his loss, and even though I tried, I couldn't seem to transcend my own pain to help him through his. I saw mother's loneliness as she tried to move past her own pain and I saw my sister's sadness as well. Andrea was very sad, and she was vying for our attention, asking questions about something she still couldn't understand. I couldn't get past my own suffering to help them, a fact that only made me feel even worse. My life had fallen apart, and I couldn't find a way out of the desolation I was in.

Each day, I fell deeper into the abyss. I decided to try to make peace so that I could reclaim my own life and move forward. With that in mind, I decided to go to the Alchichica Lagoon in Puebla to swim for a few hours to heal the wounds of my heart. I was curious to see how my body would react and determine if I was to continue with my dream of crossing the English Channel or if it would be left for another moment in life.

I remember being at the water's edge and thinking: "I am here today to find peace and begin healing a deep wound. It seems that when sadness reaches us for any reason, if we let it in, it will take ownership of our life, demanding our undivided attention and costing us our peace because of its jealous and selfish nature."

It was very painful to lose dad. He had been my friend, companion, and accomplice during our many adventures together. We always had a great time. His quiet and observant disposition was ideal when I wanted to share my hopes and dreams. He had a way of talking that helped me think twice about any decision, and there was always a compassionate smile on his face. Even though the pain cut deep, I knew that I couldn't continue feeling this way. I realized that part of the healing process was going through the pain and I needed to leave my sadness behind so that it would not dictate my actions any longer. I thought, "I want to be at peace with myself to begin enjoying life again and to be able to show my loved ones the love and support they need." With these clear intentions, I jumped into the cold waters of the Alchichica Lagoon.

I swam for three and a half hours. At first, I was fearful, sad and felt the cold water seeping into my body. My goggles were fogged up when I realized I was crying; the water was helping me let go of my pain. After a while, I looked up to the sky and saw how clear and blue it was, and with every breath, I felt a sense of calm come over me. I let the blue skies permeate my core, and with each stroke, I could see the bubbles underwater with their different sizes and shapes as I let them go behind me. I kept on swimming, feeling more and more at peace. Little by little I began recovering my serenity and enjoying myself like I usually to. I realized I was on my way again, training for the English Channel!

I was able to let go of the sadness and anguish in the wake of those bubbles and I held on to the vision of blue skies that had given me so much peace during that morning's swim. I felt myself smiling as I got out of the lagoon, reminding myself of everything father and I had lived and experienced. There had been so many incredible moments full of life and magic! His memory would forever be with me and the pain would be left behind in those waters.

I also thought of my mom while I was swimming. As I wept, still in the water, I said, "Thank you, Mom, for your happy heart and for always supporting Dad. You gave him your life and even fell off the balcony with him. You have taught me the meaning of love. Thank you!"

During my entire grief process while coping with my loss, I always had a friend's unconditional support. That friend was Gela, the same friend who swam next to me for one hour when I was crossing the English Channel.

I came back from these thoughts realizing that I had already swum many kilometers and I kept trying to see the French coast even with the waning light of sunset. However, the sky was still cloudy and gray. I could see a dark sliver of land on the horizon, but it seemed very far away. After a few moments, and when I looked up again, I remember seeing tiny flashing lights in the distance. It was getting dark and I became anxious again knowing that the temperatures would drop even more with the looming night.

I kept swimming and was able to see in the dim light that was still remaining of daytime, the message written onboard the escort ship stating: "Time to change your goggles for transparent ones!" I hadn't realized how much I needed to change my goggles for I had been using them from the start and they were too dark for me to see in the dark.

By then, my earlier emotional crisis had passed. I was still worried because I still had about three more hours to go.

Unfortunately, when Gela threw me the transparent goggles, they sank and got lost in the water. I had not choice but to continue swimming with the darker goggles that I already had on. I was hoping that Nora or Ariadna onboard would find the spare transparent goggles that I tucked away in my backpack so they could hand them over to me at the next stop. With each passing minute, it got darker. I couldn't see anything! When I raised my head towards the escort boat, I couldn't see anyone nor distinguish any of the bodies onboard. I was barely able to see a small light inside the cabin and the reflection of the light that followed me so that they wouldn't lose sight of me. When I turned my head to the other side, it was pitch black. It was also pitch black underwater, I could barely see the bubbles that my stroking arms create. Everything else was covered in darkness.

The wind picked up and I couldn't see the waves, I could only feel their movement. I tried to breathe out of the other side, trying to avoid the waves as they pushed water into my face, forcing me to swallow more seawater. I was also trying to avoid the annoying light that was reflected on me. My eyes stung horribly from so many hours of salt water seeping into my goggles. I did feel comfortable, though, being used to not seeing much around me. I was getting used to the cold, as it hadn't gotten much worse than before, a fact that kept me going forward. I couldn't see the discomfort from the cold temperatures that the crew was experiencing either. It was a welcoming bonus that kept me calm as well. My body was in tune as time kept passing by and I could tell when the thirty minutes were coming up for my next feed. I knew exactly and was ready to stop and recharge with my next warm feed. I did need those transparent goggles, though, and hoped they had been found on the boat.

Suddenly, I heard the whistle signal instructing me to stop

and approach. I took my energy drink as fast as possible, and Mike threw me a set of goggles that weren't mine. I tried to explain that they weren't mine, but before I could finish, he said emphatically, "Put them on and keep swimming!" I didn't dare disobey the order and I put them on immediately. As I continued swimming and when my head was below the water's surface, I could see a fluorescent universe underwater and it was completely different from the darkness I had experienced a few minutes prior.

I could see thousands of tiny microorganisms that shone their most vivid yellow and green incandescent fluorescent that I had ever seen. It was as if there were millions of underwater stars. The wake of my bubbles became illuminated as well. The underwater marine life was shining just for me!

By now I had been swimming for thirteen hours and I was feeling exhausted. In my last stop, I was given double the energy drink. Mike didn't want me to stop again for fear of losing time. I wasn't sure what was going on. I had seen the lights from Calais for a while but then I completely lost sight of them. I thought to myself, "Is it possible that the tides changed again with their six-hour cycle and forced me to change course because of the currents?" I didn't know how much longer I would last under these conditions. I started losing hope. I had been so close and had no idea how close I was!

I kept swimming against the current, having to put forth extra effort to keep my the pace up. I felt I was in a terrible dream where I would swim and swim without making any progress to reach my destination. This is the reality of how it is in open water swims; even if you swim with all of your might, you feel like you are not move forward at all. It takes a lot of patience to swim through those long stretches when one is training, but it becomes quite different and much more complicated when it is the real and official crossing. I was exhausted!

I had tried to be as efficient as possible, swimming at a constant pace the entire time. I had been quick at every stop – never taking longer than 30 seconds at a time. The wind was now blowing in the opposite direction and when I realized the Calais lights were nowhere in sight, I felt a great sense of loss. My goggles again filled up with tears. I had heard so many stories of swimmers who never made it to the coast of France quitting barely a mere kilometer from the shore.

I was heartbroken! A deep-rooted pain from my very core. So many months of hard training for a dream that seemed like it would never come true. I thought of my kids, of the children in need of surgeries, and about not being able to reach my goal. My entire body hurt. With each movement, the physical pain was becoming too much to bear. My eyes hurt, I had been wearing goggles for over thirteen hours, my legs hurt with each kick, my shoulders felt heavy with each stroke, and my left wrist was bothering me as well. I felt a tightness in my neck that was creeping down to my back. My throat, mouth, nose, and tongue stung so much that I couldn't swallow. My stomach ached from having swallowed so much salt water, and the pain had even affected my kidneys. But nothing compared to the pain I felt in my heart.

What must the crew be thinking? Does the situation appear different from aboard the escort boat? I couldn't tell from their expressions on their faces or tell if they felt frustration or disappointment. They couldn't see my eyes either, not even when the light shone on my face, and I don't think they were able see what I was feeling nor the huge wave of sadness that was pulling me under.

Stroke after stroke, I kept moving forward. Even though my entire body hurt, my mind had decided that I wouldn't stop until I reached the coast of France. I kept on saying to myself, "I will not get out of the water; I will not get out of the water." After a few minutes, this mantra wasn't only a wish; it had become a command that my brain was sending to my entire body. Even when the current kept pulling me off course, I kept on swimming. I still couldn't understand what happened to the lights from the coastline and why I couldn't see them anymore.

I looked to the crew, asking for an explanation, and they said that I was still about a kilometer and a half away. My heart skipped a beat when I heard Gela rooting me on and telling me that the worst part was over. Nora explained that I was getting very close but would have to double my efforts and swim against the current. I still had no sight of the coastline, but I would continue on without stopping.

Not being able to see the French coastline lights still baffled me. Just as I had lost sight of those lights in what seemed like an instant, when I turned my head, I was able to see from the corner of my eye how a majestic bright moon had suddenly appeared! I had been swimming in the dark for a few hours and had not seen it until now.

It was around eleven at night, and the moon kept popping out from behind the clouds - illuminating the crests of the waves with its bright light. I enjoy swimming in the moonlight, which gave me a much needed distraction from the uncertainty that I felt when I wasn't able to see the coastline. I had been swimming for four hours in the dark and up until a few moments ago I was able to see the moon. It was almost as if it was trying to remind me of something important. "A tiny jar of moon air keeps me from drowning, to not give up and keep on going!"

I continued swimming, forcing every fiber in my body to give me the necessary energy and strength to complete the swim. When I looked back at the escort boat, I saw Nora standing on the railing with her bathing suit on ready to jump in the water. She explained quickly that we were close to the coast but would be arriving at a beach that was far from Calais, and she would swim alongside me to guide me in the correct direction. I understood then why I hadn't been able to see the lights from the shore - we had changed course to another beach. I had already swum past Calais!

How do I explain what I was feeling? I don't know how to describe my feelings at that moment. On the one hand, each movement was painful, my heart rate was erratic, and it took a tremendous amount of effort to breathe. My body couldn't take much more, but my head forced me to keep going on.

On the other hand, I felt hope that my dream was indeed achievable. I began swimming next to Nora. She was swimming fast, and I was trying to keep up with her, but I knew I couldn't keep up this pace for long. But I also thought that if she was in the water, reaching the coastline would take 20-40 minutes at most. The previous night, Captain Mike Oram had explained that if the weather conditions were favorable, a Zodiac would take the judge and crew to accompany me on the last few meters to the beach. But if the wind and conditions were dangerous, Nora would swim beside me on that last stretch, and the boat would remain three or four hundred meters from the coast.

I was swimming my last few meters of the English Channel!

My body had reached its limit of cold, pain, and exhaustion, but my mind began playing scenes of my family celebrating. I could see my friends and also the children who would benefit from the donations coming from this incredible effort. All of these people had been the motivation that kept me swimming. But above all, I felt immense love for my kids: Lalo and Andrea.

I stopped for a moment and saw that the boat was illuminating the beach. I felt my feet touch the sand! I had arrived! Nothing would hold me back from reaching France. I was less than half a kilometer away. I swam those last 200 meters of the English Channel crying but didn't stop until my hands touched the sand. In order for the challenge to be considered valid, I had to get out of the water. But as I tried to stand on my feet, the waves kept pulling me back, and I fell. I began crawling, moving to the shore and tried to get up again. My body was at its limit, but so were my emotions. I was still crying, feeling happiness, pain, and exhaustion all at the same time. I got out of the water with much difficulty, barely keeping my balance. I took a few steps and raised my arms in victory. With my arms in the air, I heard the horn signal from the escort boat which marked the successful end to my journey. I lowered myself to pick up a pebble stone from this side of the English Channel. I had done it! I closed my eyes and felt a strong and heartfelt hug from my Dad.

The official time was 14 hours and 33 minutes. I swam 57 kilometers from the coast of England to the coast of France, but more than the distance covered, I swam my life on that journey. It felt as if I had swum an ocean of commitment, will, love, and passion. Andrea's words on the dock had been prophetic when she commanded saying, "Mom, make sure you finish, huh?" And that's exactly what I did... I finished it! I did it!

Crossing the English Channel represented so much more than covering the distance between Dover and Calais. I swam without stopping, resting, assistance, or good weather conditions. The cold, wind, waves, and tides had pushed me to limits I never knew I could attain. It meant having to travel many kilometers, not only measured in physical terms but also measured emotionally because I faced pain, sadness, fortitude, empathy, love, friendship, and finally, peace.

CHAPTER 4
THE COVID-19 VIRUS

So many memories! When the pilot finally announced our descent, I came back to reality. I became aware of what was happening in the world at large. The threat of a virus was so powerful that it was transforming the world.

Upon landing in the International Airport of Mexico City, I was faced with a situation that made a strong impact on me. Very different from that which I experienced in Buenos Aires, this airport was open as usual, as if there was no COVID-19 virus at all. The stores and restaurants were open, there were tons of people everywhere, and the Mexican authorities assured us that there wasn't anything to worry about. Even the President announced that everything was under control and that we should not isolate ourselves from family and friends. However, something was amiss. International news were alarming in the rest of the world. Most countries outside of Mexico were already enforcing quarantine measures and mandatory use of mask. We were constantly informed about death rates among infected victims.

When I got home, my children didn't come close to greet me. They didn't hug me and asked that I self-quarantine myself in my bedroom for fifteen days as a preventive measure just in case I contracted the virus during my trip. Their attitude took me aback, and I was doubtful if it was really necessary for me to isolate myself in my room. However, I did, I remembered what I had already experienced in Buenos Aires.

During those fifteen days in isolation, I became aware of the gravity of the situation. I began understanding the real meaning of the word "pandemic." I could hardly believe the negative impact that resulted from the virus mismanagement by the authorities in my country. It saddened me deeply to learn that thousands of cases that were not being taken care of and about the many doctors and nurses who were battling against all odds to help treat the sick. Many people who had contracted the virus searched desperately for any aid, and as a result, many died without having been given the necessary care.

With the passing of days, more people caught the virus. Some survived the illness at home, while others needed medical attention from hospitals and health centers. How ever, the latter lacked the capacity to treat the many patients who sought out treatment on a daily basis. Many horror stories became public – people who died in waiting rooms, nurses who got the virus because they lacked the necessary protection gear, funeral homes that could not attend to the many bodies, and many people in panic who searched for the necessary equipment to keep at home in case of an emergency.

The elderly population was the most vulnerable, as well as people who suffered from chronic illness and those who came from low-income backgrounds. These people lived under constant stress watching the rate at which the COVID-19 virus was spreading around the country. Pregnant women also worried about their health and the health of their babies - each day, their fear turned into panic, and we were all living in a state of distress.

During my confinement, I reminisced about the time when I had crossed the Catalina Channel. It was a challenge to swim in these waters because it implied many hours swimming at night, and this caused me much anxiety and fear within me.

"I could see nothing but the tiny stars shining under water that formed constellations similar to the ones we observe in the night sky.

The darker the depths of water, the brighter the plankton shone. It was like a rainfall of tiny shooting stars that passed in front of my eyes, shining for an instant just for me."

Catalina Channel, August 2013.

CHAPTER 5
CATALINA CHANNEL

The Catalina Channel can be found between the Island of Santa Catalina and the coast of California, close to Palos Verdes and Long Beach. In its most narrow stretch it is about 34 kilometers wide and the water temperature typically ranges between 15ºC to 17ºC (59ºF - 63ºF) during Spring and between 19ºC to 22ºC (66ºF - 72ºF) during Summer. My swim was scheduled for the 24th or 25th of August, beginning in Catalina Island and finishing in Palos Verdes, California. This swim usually begins at midnight because strong winds pick up during the day, making it difficult for a swimmer to stay on course. During my training, I swam in Las Estacas, Morelos, and the Alchichica Lagoon in Puebla – similar to the training that I underwent through my preparation to crossing the English Channel.

I still recall that as the trip got closer, I began to feel a sense of insecurity and restlessness. I would try to keep those negative thoughts at bay, but even though I succeeded in forgetting for a few days, they would return inevitably to continue plaguing me. With the month of August looming closer, so did the negative thoughts becoming more intense. The days came and went quickly with my daily routine: taking care of children, my job, and household chores. I kept busy training, as I felt most at ease while I was in the water. I was confident that my training was adequate; however, I couldn't stop worrying, and this kept me from sleeping well at night. I would get tense whenever I thought about the upcoming challenge. I tried not to think about it, but it was difficult because the trip was getting closer with each passing day.

One evening, after a long day of training and a thousand different errands, I went to bed early but woke up screaming a few hours later. I had a terrible nightmare. I was terrified! In my dream, I was swimming in a red sea, with floating body parts and lots of blood around me. A fin above water was circling around me. I understood the root cause of my anxiety: I was afraid of sharks!

I became aware that during the past few nights, I had many other nightmares that would wake me up, and it would take me a long time to be able to fall back asleep. I stopped watching the Discovery Channel, which broadcasted a show called "Shark Week." I didn't even want to see advertisements for the movie "Nemo" because it showed a huge smiling shark with sharp teeth and a menacing look.

During those previous months, people had asked me directly if I was afraid of sharks, while others merely looked at me in silence. This topic became more frequent as the date drew closer and closer. A week before traveling to California, while I was training in Sport City, a swimmer asked me what event I was training for. When I told him it was training to swim the Catalina Channel, he said, "Hey Mariel, did you know that the Catalina Channel is famous for being a zone for white sharks?" I was so taken aback that I didn't know what to answer back.

That evening, my anxiety got the best of me, and I broke down crying, full of fear and worry. I didn't know what to do. I asked myself if it was worth it. Was I taking an unnecessary risk? I was so confused! The night seemed to pass away at a snail's pace, but when dawn broke, I finally began to relax. I thought of all the people who had already swum the Channel and had left the waters unscathed. I was still uncertain if I should cancel, so many conflicting thoughts ran through my head. Finally, I was able to sleep for a couple of hours; I was so tired that day. However, in the light of day, I saw things quite differently and decided I wouldn't cancel my trip!

A few days later, I made it to Long Beach, California, with my support crew: Nora, Gela, and Ariadna. I still felt a weight on my shoulders, and even though I tried to control my fears, they plagued me constantly. I decided not to train that afternoon and walked along the beach instead. I tried to leave my worries behind, reflecting on why I was so scared. I thought of those who are afraid of flying. The chances of an airplane accident are minimal, and even so, they are terrified while other passengers are at ease, some even drifting off into a peaceful sleep during flight.

A friend of mine from Uruguay who enjoys surfing once told me, "Mariel, when I am in the water, and I think of sharks, one suddenly appears, and I am forced to get out of the water. When I don't think about them, they never appear." And then I also recalled what Captain John Pittman had said during a phone conversation, "If you are scared, spit your fear into a jar, close it, and throw it away. Don't bring it along on your swims because those feelings do not help you at all." I decided to do just that – I spat my fear and let it go.

On Friday, August 24th, at 8:00 pm, we boarded the Outridder, and the adventure began. My first challenge was not to get seasick on the trip from Long Beach to Catalina Island, which took almost three and a half hours. It was important to feel well to be ready to swim. When we reached the starting point, a little before 11:30 pm, Nora and Gela helped me get ready: Vaseline under the bathing suit straps, Lassar cream under the armpits, sunscreen for when the sun came out, along with other needed preparations.

It was dark outside; I couldn't see anything! We were about 150 meters from the shore, and I couldn't even see the reflection of the waves on the water. Everything around us was pitch black, but I felt fine and ready to jump in the water. On the boat ride to Catalina Island, we had a safety briefing with John Pittman and the rest of the crew. John said something that helped me relax, "We will do everything in our power to make sure your swim is successful. Your safety will always be priority number one." It was exactly what I needed to hear at that moment!

When I was ready to jump in, the judge that would supervise me, dearest Anne Cleveland (may she rest in peace -

who surely is a mermaid of energy filling all the oceans on the planet), said, "Jump in the water and enjoy! Swim towards the beach, get out of the water, and ignore the seals that get close to you. We don't want you to waste any time playing with the baby seals that are curious by nature. And as soon as you are ready, lift up your arms, the horn from the boat will sound, and at that moment, you will begin your swim to the California coast. Try to hang on in the darkness, for once the sun begins to rise, things will get easier. There is much life in these waters. Enjoy the experience!"

The last thing that had ever occurred to me was to play with seals!

Before jumping in the water, and as a way to prolong the inevitable, I thanked my team: Nora, Gela, and Ariadna; Javier Gutiérrez, a fellow swimmer and friend who had joined us last minute; Anne and Theo, her assistant. My two kayakers, Kim and Don, would follow beside me and the rest of the crew. And once the moment arrived, I jumped headfirst into the darkest, blackest sea I had ever seen.

I swam quickly, trying to reach the spot that the boat was illuminating. There was a lot of kelp, forcing me to keep my head up above water, and I got out of the ocean as fast as I could so that I could get started as soon as possible. Everything was pitch black around me; I had no idea if they were rocks or sleeping seals around me. I lifted my arms up to the sky and thanked God, asking for his protection. At that instant, I heard the horn signal. As a good luck charm, I picked up a small pebble, put it inside my bathing suit, and began swimming!

During the seven hours I swam that night, I was able to see the vibrant marine life shining every time I my head was underwater. The nocturnal creatures shone like tiny stars, forming constellations like those in the sky. The darker it was outside, the brighter the plankton seemed to glow for me. It was like a shower of shooting stars passing in front of my eyes, reminding me of the love from people like my dad and grandparents who were no longer with us. Other than the light from the plankton, I couldn't see anything else. I could feel the fish brushing next to my body, the jellyfish that would try and sting me, and the different-sized medusas that touched me as I passed them by. I felt special and unique because of these bright stars that surrounded me in this underwater nocturnal universe. I didn't need to see anything; I was swimming with my heart!

When the sun came up, my eyes were witness to the plentiful life in the Catalina Channel and its blue waters. The beautiful color of the Pacific Ocean, a hue between green and deep blue, motivated me to keep swimming towards the coast. I didn't feel alone during the hours I swam in daylight. Gela kept me company with her enthusiasm, and I kept up the pace even when I was tired. Then, dozens of dolphins came along to visit and reminded me that this journey would result in one hundred surgeries for children with CLP. Towards the end of my crossing, Javier joined me swimming all the way to the rocks in Terranea, Palos Verdes. It took me 11 hours and 27 minutes to swim the 34 kilometers of the Catalina Channel, and I never felt any fear at all!

I climbed out of the water and hiked up some slippery rocks. The waves kept me from making it to solid ground, but even though it was difficult, I was able to climb out. I had a huge smile on my face just knowing that I was the first Mexican woman to complete this challenge, and with that, I had become the 61st person in the world to accomplish the Triple Crown of Open Water Swimming: English Channel (33 km), Catalina Channel (33 km), and 20 Bridges Swim around Manhattan Island (48.5 km).

Do you know how I swam the Catalina Channel? I did it with all my heart - just as the Fox, from my favorite book, The Little Prince, by Antoine de Saint Exupery, always says: "One cannot see well except with the heart; the essential is invisible to the eyes." And above all, I did it, leaving all my fears behind!

"Some say that it is imperative to train like the best in order to be a champion, but I say one must train like the best, even in the worst moments, and one must give it all even in those days of pain and uncertainty."

Mexico City, February 2015.

CHAPTER 6
THE HURRICANE OF MY LIFE

During the first weeks of my confinement because of the COVID-19 pandemic, I was filled with much anguish and uncertainty.

I wasn't actually feeling fear but felt very apprehensive at the thought of leaving the house. Once the two weeks of self-quarantine (after returning from my trip to Argentina) were over, it was inevitable to go out and buy supplies. I didn't have face masks, so I called my local pharmacy to get some delivered. I was alarmed at the salesperson's response: they weren't open to the public and were out of face masks. He went on to ask me if I wanted to be placed on a very long waitlist.

The following day, after a sleepless night and feeling significantly more anxious, I made my own face mask made out of many layers of fabric scraps I found lying around the house. I made my way out to buy groceries at a nearby 24-hour supermarket. I arrived at the store at 5:30 am and was completely astonished at what I encountered at the grocery store. There were only a handful of employees, and the ones that were there were dressed in full protective gear with face masks, gloves, and plastic eye goggles. You could barely see their faces. It was surreal as if it were a scene from a science fiction movie. Customers were not allowed to get close to the employees and they, in turn, avoided touching any of the merchandize. All purchases had to be paid for using a credit card. Face masks were sold out, and many other common household goods were also unavailable. I bought what I could get for the next few weeks, hoping the situation would improve in time. I had no idea what would happen and little did I know what was in store for me and the rest of the world.

On my way back home, the sky took on a rosy and orange hue as the sun came out. In the horizon, I could clearly see the Popocatepetl and Iztaccihuatl volcanoes, as if they were larger and closer than usual - majestic at a distance. Mexico City was waking up.

I felt a lump in my throat as I realized it was another day amid the pandemic. I began to cry, tears of anguish, unable to breathe, and feeling desolate at the impotence of doing anything for those who had contracted the virus and were in a precarious situation as their life began to fade away.

I got home and couldn't shake the feeling that I had possibly been infected during my outing, so I remained in the car without knowing what to do next. As I sat in the car, I had a vision of many memories, specifically about a moment on a Monday morning in mid-April 2014...

Those memories meant going back to one of the most painful moments in my life and exposing myself again to those wounds, drowning in a sea of emotions that would take me to relive the many miles of sadness and pain. I leave this story written here for you in case you may also be going through a similar ocean of emotions so that you may find solace even amongst the most stormy of days. And even if you cannot see how this uncertainty will end, always remember that the tide always changes, and in its process, the end result is transformation.

That early Monday morning, I received a call at the office. It was from the security office in the building letting me know that a neighbor had reported that the front door to my apartment had been left open, and no one seemed to be at home. It felt very strange! At first, I thought I had forgotten to close the door on my way out that morning. But I then remembered that Eduardo had stayed behind after I left for work and that seemed completely out of character because he never forgets to lock up the door behind him. I called him at work, but he couldn't remember if he had locked the door behind him or not. It seemed like Eduardo didn't give much importance to that situation.

A few days later, during dinner, a conversation with the children ensued. But Eduardo seemed distracted and wasn't paying much attention to the conversation. I thought maybe he was under pressure at work, but his behavior seemed out of character for him because he was always vested in spending quality time with us when we were together and enjoyed hearing Lalo and Andrea talk about their day and other details. During the following weeks, Eduardo kept acting differently, very quiet and distracted, with moments of distraction and feeling very tired. We decided to see a doctor for these symptoms, and on April 29th, 2014, we got the results back. As the doctor explained the test results, I felt a hurricane of emotions explode inside me!

"Eduardo has a malignant brain tumor," the doctor told us.

Upon hearing this diagnosis, I felt like I couldn't breathe. I was sitting in the doctor's office, and my heart began beat ing so fast I thought it would jump out of my chest. I tried to calm down my breathing; I felt as if I was choking and as if I was in the middle of a hurricane. My world began to spin, and I couldn't make it stop.

I tried to keep calm and to have faith. I wanted to feel at peace and not feel the anguish I was experiencing after hearing the news. As the doctor continued on and explained the available treatments, I was able to relax, and I took Eduardo's hand, telling him, "You are not alone; I am right here."

When we left the doctor's office, I told Eduardo that from that day on, my shoulders, which had been strengthened because of the hundreds of kilometers that I had swum, would be his to lean on going forward.

We told the kids what was happening, and they were filled with fear. Fear usually paralyzes us and robs us of the ability to live, enjoy, and dream. I was at a loss on how I should act in this situation. We were experiencing deep pain, fear, and anxiety, and our world was collapsing all around us.

Eduardo was very brave and when I saw his positive attitude, I remembered a phrase my father used to say, "Fill your mind with hope and will, and your heart with love and happiness, so that fear will tremble and leave your life and allow you to move on."

However, there are moments in life when, no matter how hard you try to follow this advice, you are stuck in the middle of a whirlwind with no clear way out.

A few days after learning the diagnosis, Eduardo went in for his first surgery. The children and I went along with him all the way to the entry of the operating room. We kissed him and reminded him that he wasn't alone. The doctor had explained that this surgery would take about 5 to 6 hours. At the end of the procedure, Eduardo would remain hospitalized for a few days, and he would then continue his recovery at home, after which he would receive radiation and chemotherapy. He was administered the strongest doses of radiation available, and during the entire process, Eduardo kept a positive attitude. I tried to mirror his good humor and enthusiasm, especially in front of the kids. The days and months passed quickly, with only thoughts of his recovery in mind.

At the end of July, Eduardo's prognosis was a good one, and the doctor told him he could once again go back and live a normal everyday life. With that information, we planned a trip to Acapulco for that coming November to swim the renowned challenge called "El Reto", which translates into English as "The Challenge."

On Saturday, November 8th, 2014, my two children and I participated in "El Reto," which consists of swimming 6.5 kilometers in Acapulco. We swam in support of "Casa de Amistad para Niños con cancer (IAP)," or "The House of Friendship for Children with Cancer." We would raise enough money to donate blankets and other basic necessities for these children who were receiving treatment for their disease. We felt honored to help other families going through a situation similar to our own.

My son Lalo, who was fourteen at the time, had already completed the "El Reto" challenge back in 2010, so the days before the event, he felt quite relaxed. However, Andrea was about to turn fourteen and was going to participate in this challenge for the first time, feeling very nervous about doing so. She was also excited! I decided to swim beside her so she felt my company during the journey.

On the day of the event, we woke up knowing that it would be a day filled with love for Eduardo, who would accompany us the entire trip from aboard the escort boat. The event takes place from the Naval Base of Icacos to La Marina, a yacht club in Acapulco. The three of us began together, swimming towards the goal. And as we came up to breathe, we would see each other and Eduardo as well from aboard the boat. Eventually, Lalo took off swimming at his own pace, joining other swimmers up ahead. Andrea and I stayed behind, swimming together. It took us almost three hours to cross the bay of Santa Lucia. We swam side by side, loving each other more with each stroke. It seemed as if we were mirroring our moves, and as we made eye contact, we kept silent. I saw all the love in the world in Andrea's eyes. In her left eye, she has a light birthmark, a mark of light, and in her eyes, I saw the reflection of an entire universe. Swimming by her side was like gliding through the universe together.

It isn't easy to swim for three continuous hours in open waters. In addition, Andrea's training hadn't really been enough for this challenge. Even so, her perseverance and strength to continue despite her exhaustion took me by surprise. I could see that the straps of her bathing suit had chafed her skin, and she was forced to put in more effort to continue on stroke after stroke. In spite of this, she never gave up, which only proved that Andrea was made of, using a very colloquial phrase from my country, a very strong wood!

We finished the swim together and as we got out of the water Lalo welcomed us with the best price and recognition we could have ever asked for. He had completed the swim an hour before! Eduardo also waited for us and gave us the best hug. When we got close to the shore, he went ahead on the boat to be there waiting for us with open arms.

That day, Andrea crossed the Acapulco Bay swimming, growing up and maturing in ways which allowed her to leave the young innocent girl behind, transforming her into the wonderful young woman she is today. A young girl who understands that life is to be lived with a smile because the magic of her smile lights up everyone's spirit even the darkest days. Not only that, but Andrea also learned that life never stops and that her effort affects not only herself but the people around her; her strokes as she navigates life can help transform the lives of others as well.

That evening, during the awards ceremony, Andrea stood

up when they called out her name, took a deep breath, and before she walked towards the stage, she turned to look at her father. At that moment, their eyes met, and time stood still - all of the love, complicity, and magic between a father and daughter crystallized at that precise moment. Through that look, they lived an eternity together.

Andrea moved to the front to receive her diploma without taking her eyes off Eduardo. He knew at that moment that his daughter had accomplished much more than he ever imagined, and it was her way of showing her love for him. That night, Eduardo and Andrea shared a special moment. Their love will remain forever as an eternal pact between father and daughter.

Lalo, Andrea, and I swam "El Reto," full of faith and enjoying every moment because we understood that even in the midst of a storm, we can swim through anything. With each stroke and kick in the water, we were able to show our love and unrelenting support for Eduardo!

In December 2014, a few days after the "El Reto" challenge, Eduardo had his second surgery. His tumor came back into our lives, leaving destruction and loss in its path.

The uncertainty of it all was overwhelming, and Eduardo's health was critical. Even so, I was certain that this surgery would get rid of the tumor.

A few days before the second surgical intervention, I woke up convinced that even though life poses us with difficult situations, we must learn to handle the anxiety and continue on our path forward, finding a sense of calm and remaining strong. This is necessary as we support others and, specifically in this case, support for Eduardo and our children.

Just as exceptional athletes train each day to give their best, we should all prepare for life's difficulties. Some say that it is imperative to train like the best to be a champion, but I say one must train like the best, even in the worst moments and give it all even in those days where one feels pain and uncertainty.

The surgery was a success; however, the cancer didn't stop spreading in Eduardo's brain. I was really scared and I didn't know how to express my feelings - I didn't speak about my fears with anyone since everyone expected me to be strong, especially for my kids. I felt like if I were drowning because I was keeping my silence buried deep within me while I kept thinking: "This hurricane is sweeping me and my family, and I can't see past my pain and its destruction as it keeps pulling me under."

The MRI that Eduardo had three weeks after the surgery showed new and aggressive cancerous cells once again. I couldn't believe it! Not even a month had passed by and already a new tumor was growing. I wanted to run away screaming until I had no voice left, expecting to stop the physical pain I was in. Up to this point, Eduardo had been brave and strong during the entire process, but I feared that the news of yet another cancerous tumor would be devastating to him. He had been so certain that this surgery would finally eradicate his cancer. I was afraid he would not react positively to the news that the cancer had come back.

In February 2015, he underwent his third surgery. It was another test of life and resilience and, just as before, Eduardo was a beacon of optimism and enthusiasm. As we waited for him to enter the operating room, he showed no fear. This helped put the kids at ease. This time, however, the recovery was very different from the past surgeries. He underwent many hours of physical therapy and had to regain abilities he had lost on the left side of his body. In reality, the cancer continue spreading at an aggressive rate.

On February 11th, 2015, a few days after the third surgery, and while he was still in rehabilitation, we celebrated our twentieth anniversary. We looked into each other's eyes, saying so much in that moment without speaking a word. We also sat down to discuss many unspoken truths we didn't want to face in the past few years. Some of the things he told me surprised me. Others were flattering and some were painful. He held me in his arms and we cried together.

"Let's keep it up, Mom! We have to keep swimming strong until we get to Morocco!

Those last few meters I was able to enjoy the color of the ocean and swim next to Lalo until we touched the African coast, hugging each other as we got out of the water in Punta Almansa, Morocco."

Strait of Gibraltar, July 2015

CHAPTER 7
THE STRAIT OF GIBRALTAR

March 2015 came quickly and with it the tides from the Strait of Gibraltar. A few weeks after Eduardo's surgery, at the beginning of March, the cancer was spreading without any respite and without giving him any time to recover.

Up until that moment, I had always believed that things would work out if one does the right things. I always held on to the belief that good things happen to good people. But life would show me a very different outcome - and things don't always work out the way one expects. I cried constantly not only because I deeply worried about Eduardo's health and anguish I felt to taking care of my children, but also because I felt completely betrayed by life. What I had known to be true in the past was no longer so, which confirmed that even though I had tried to do things the right way, things did not work out for us. I tried to be good and act with kindness, but this felt so unfair to me. I couldn't believe I was ready to give up. It isn't easy to see how, little by little, life is coming to an end for the one person you love. The pain chokes you up and oppresses you, even more so when that person is my husband and the father of my children.

As Eduardo's health worsened, each one of us was dying a little bit. It was the pain I saw in my children's eyes that made me realize that we were all losing a part of ourselves in the process. I broke down, I couldn't stop crying, and I can't recall how long it took me to regain my composure. I was reaching my limit and couldn't take much more of it. There was a thunderstorm outside and the thunder and lightning shook the ground which moved me to action. I had a clear reminder of something I knew to be true: "Even if lightning strikes and threatens to break you in two parts, the decision to allow it to do so is yours alone." The impact of that thunder strike shifted the feelings of fear and pain, making room for the promise that things would be alright.

The following morning, Lalo broke down and told me he didn't have the strength to live with the sadness he was experiencing witnessing dad´s suffering. I told him that from that moment on, we would give him all the love and support we could. I still had faith that Eduardo would recover from his third surgery as the days would go by. I thought that we would be able to travel to Spain that coming summer, as planned. When I saw the weight and sadness that Lalo was carrying, I asked him to swim the Strait of Gibraltar with me and as a result of this request, I was able to see a bright new light in his eyes full of excitement. He said, "Yes, Mom, I want to swim the Strait of Gibraltar as a way to honor dad."

I hugged him with all my might. In that instant, I knew I had planted a seed in him that could grow into something wonderful. That seed was the certainty that his father would get better and that together (including Eduardo and Andrea aboard the boat), we would swim the Strait of Gibraltar in the coming months. At the end of that day, I knew that even though the thunder and lightning had the power to destroy and split us in two, its strength could also renew our faith and desire that everything would get better. It would allow our inner strength to give us the motivation to move forward, with unwavering conviction that everything would be alright.

Soon enough, it was already April. I read a book about how our children grow so fast that before you know it they become adolescents and in mere instances, they would next experience adulthood. The author wrote about daily situations that he had shared with his children and how, at certain times, he experienced feelings of emptiness and sadness as he watched his kids reach adulthood.

My children also had matured in a very short period of time. They had been forced to experience many painful and complicated situations due to Eduardo´s sickness and the death of their grandfather. During those nights, watching over Eduardo, I thought of Lalo and Andrea's childhood. We shared all of the amazing moments, from the crazy mornings rushing to school to the afterschool classes and evening dinnertime as a family (many nights without saying much because we were exhausted). I also remembered sunny days filled with water, laughter, fun, hugs, games, and thousands of emotions that can only be attributed to love.

Being by Eduardo's side during his illness was a test of will for all of us. In my children's case, they had been forced to mature at an accelerated pace. From one moment to the next, they felt the pressure to grow up, as if the cancer challenged them to move forward quickly. That is exactly how it had been; they moved along with their pain, carrying moments with faith to embrace the future.

As we began to train for the Strait of Gibraltar, one weekend, Lalo and I went to a swim meet for masters at Mexico's National University campus in Mexico City. At one moment during the meet, I saw Lalo walking along the border of the pool. He was "accompanying" an octogenarian who was swimming the 100-meter, cheering him all the way. When the competitor finally made it to the other side, Lalo burst into a round of applause and everyone in the pool and the stands joined him in the celebration. I was, in reality, also applauding Lalo for his incredible empathy!

After a little while, a good friend of mine named Rosaura Hernandez (category 80+- may she rest in peace) came closer to tell me, "Did you see that young, good-looking young man in the orange t-shirt? He helped me get out of the pool after my challenge. He is such a gentleman." She was talking about Lalo…My Lalo!

Andrea also matured during this time - growing emotionally, much more so than her height. I organized a family gathering where we prayed together for Eduardo's recovery. Andrea stood up and led the prayer in a way that moved me. She prayed with so much faith as an adult and asked God to bless everyone present. Her maturity in this moment only confirmed to us all how much she had grown.

Andrea's prayer prepared us for April 29th. Much in the same way where a new day starts at dawn and ends at dusk; in one moment we are born and in the next moment we are gone. Life and death are both beyond our control and just like that, the day came when Eduardo was finally laid to rest in eternal peace. His passing didn't come as a surprise to us, but it did cause us an immense amount of pain.

He woke up with a smile, probably knowing this would be his last day. His smile reminded me of the thousands of happy moments we had shared since the day we met in college, and from there on, every single day we spent together we talked and shared dreams and adventures. I thought of his zest for life, his happy disposition, enthusiasm, commitment to his work, days together on vacation when Lalo and Andrea were little and all those moments filled with mutual support, love, and complicity. His smile that morning was his way of quietly and peacefully saying goodbye. His smile also showed all his love and his eyes shone in a way that made me know he had a star that would carry his name forever, knowing where he was going and being able to visualize the best path to get there.

A few days before, his eyes had seemed empty. Ever since the third intervention, his body had deteriorated so much and it was painful to watch how the cancer was taking a toll on him. He would spend most of his days sleeping, and during the few hours he was awake, he would stare into space while our kids and I did everything to show him our love. However, as I said before, he woke up smiling that morning. He held on to me with one hand and to Andrea with the other. Lalo held on to him in a warm embrace. His face seemed serene, and his eyes shone brightly without any trace of pain; he seemed completely at peace. Andrea laid down next to him on the other side to hold him along with Lalo. His parents and brothers came to see him that day to show him their love. We were all by Eduardo's side as he passed away. With my left hand gently caressing his face and with my right palm holding onto his hand, I will always carry with me his last breath…his last breath that turned into an eternal smile.

Even though Eduardo passed away peacefully, we were left with the sensation that a hurricane had passed by destroying everything in its path. We felt desolate, sad, angry, and without knowing what to do, literally drowning in our lives. I spent many days filled with a deep-rooted pain that wouldn't let me be, without any sense of time, and unable to keep track of what day it was. One day finally, Lalo approached me and said, "Mom, I want to swim Gibraltar. I want to do it in Dad's memory!" I felt so overwhelmed during my grief process that I truly believed I would never swim again. My immediate answer was: "Lalo, there is no way. I don't ever want to swim again!" But Lalo answered, "I promised Dad. Let's go and swim it together!" And so it was Lalo that helped me return to the water. The training we endured to get ready for Gibraltar helped us get through our pain and sadness. It became our way to come together as a family and overcome our grief.

Our plane trip took over ten hours from Mexico to Spain, with an additional five-hour layover in Madrid. We then flew to Malaga and drove approximately 2 hours to Tarifa. Upon arriving in Tarifa at 10:30 pm, we had been traveling for twenty-four hours. It was then when we received the news that the weather and strait conditions would allow us to swim the following day starting between 9:30 and 10:30 am.

At 2:00 in the morning, I was still awake thinking about everything the three of us were about to begin with this upcoming challenge. I barely slept that night, a mere few hours of restless sleep. I felt pressured and anxious about what was to come. I felt at a loss knowing that we didn't even have a day to rest after the journey to adapt to the jet lag or in the schedule. I was worried about Lalo, for he was surely as tired as I was and still groping with jet lag. I also worried about Andrea, who would board the escort boat and might feel sick as she sailed with the crew that would accompany us on the swim. I tossed and turned worrying about all these swimming thoughts until I finally fell asleep most likely during the early morning hours. When I woke up, I realized that I had only slept a couple of hours. I suddenly realized the weight and magnitude of what was to happen in just a few hours: the challenge to swim the Strait of Gibraltar!

When we reached the docks to board the escort boat and begin this new adventure, I could feel Lalo's nervous energy, but not as much as mine. Anyone could see on his face how worried he really was. It wasn't something to be taken lightly—I was about to swim from Europe to Africa with my son. It encompassed open water swimming, and that can throw anyone into a nervous fit! This time my support crew would be Paty Kohlmann, a great friend and swimmer who was in Tarifa by chance, along with Gela and Andrea. Toño Argüelles and Nora would also swim along with us.

Everything was ready and in a few minutes we would board the escort boat to begin the swim at the European starting point. Those moments prior to getting started became emotionally unbearable. All four of us about to start swimming huddled up and Toño said the precise words I needed to hear at that moment, "I suggest we all swim at the same pace. That way, we can support Lalo on his way to completing the Strait of Gibraltar challenge." With these words, I saw Lalo smile. It helped him relax and my watery eyes filled with unshed tears; I felt moved at witnessing how Lalo overcame adversity and was ready to face the challenge.

We sailed a short distance to our starting point. Before jumping in the water, I hugged Andrea and Lalo and told them that this swim would be to honor their father.

Once I was in the water, I felt a surge of emotions and started to cry. I was overwhelmed by the conflicting emotions

I was feeling at that moment. However, I got them under control, knowing that I would need to be emotionally centered for the swim. Halfway through, I became worried about Lalo; I thought he might not be able to finish. I was so worried that I didn't realize how well he was doing. Once we were close to finishing, I noticed that Toño and Nora had stopped a little up ahead of me and Lalo. I also saw Lalo. When we caught up to them, Toño said, "Mariel, why don't you and Lalo swim ahead." Lalo understood at once and said, "Come on, Mom! Let's give it our all and make it to Morocco." Those last few meters, I was able to enjoy the sea's color and swim beside Lalo until we both reached the African coast. When we got out of the water in Punta Almansa, Morocco, we embraced each other in a warm hug and cried together.

This swim meant so much for Lalo. Not only did he honor his father's memory, but he could complete the project they had shared when he was alive.

A few minutes later, Toño and Nora also reached the coastline. The four of us lifted up our arms in a sign of our victory. We had crossed the Strait of Gibraltar in four hours and twenty-three minutes.

It had been a spectacular journey! The sky was beautiful, and the sun had shone the entire time. Lalo and I had enjoyed each other's company in the water, which had motivated us to make it to Morocco. With the support from Gela and Paty aboard the escort boat, we felt assured that everything would be ok. But we most enjoyed Andrea's constant cheers and shouts of encouragement that helped us along and the way as Lalo completed the challenge--amazing!

We sailed back to Tarifa and celebrated with a delicious dinner as we watched the sunset. I was exhausted from the physical effort but also because of the strenuous trip and lack of sleep. I was exhausted! I couldn't keep my eyes open, and I just wanted to go to bed and sleep.

As soon as I got to my hotel, I fell into a deep and restorative sleep for many hours. I woke up to the call to prayer that could be heard from the loudspeakers around the city. I could hear a melodic voice singing that was actually calling the devout to pray and express their gratitude. I am not Muslim, but that call to prayer awakened me from the lethargic state I had been in for the past ten hours.

Suddenly, I became aware that I had dreamt it all. There hadn't been any call to prayer! Anyhow, I got up and sent up a prayer of gratitude for that new day.

I stepped out onto the balcony and rubbed my eyes to see better; what I saw before me seemed unreal. A fire, with a red flaming ball over the ocean, seemed to hang above the water. It was a beautiful sunrise! The sunrise colored the clouds and water in pink hues and colored the daybreak with brush strokes of orange. It served as a reminder that after darkness comes light, and this light filled my soul with warmth and illuminated my path. I closed my eyes and prayed with all my heart and soul.

In the midst of the early morning silence, I gave thanks for this sunrise and for the wonderful blessing of being alive. At that moment, I thought about the difficult moments our family had survived during the past months. I let go of those sad thoughts and decided to express my gratitude instead. I gave thanks for my life and for my children, for my parents, my sister, my nephews, and my close friends, all who gave me their love and support during my time of need. I felt tears on my cheeks, but they evaporated with the touch of the sun upon my face. Just as the tears had disappeared, I felt sadness leave my body as the beauty of that sunrise overcame me. I could clearly see the Strait of Gibraltar with the morning rays of sunlight. I was able to understand that after swimming for four hours and twenty-three minutes beside Lalo and with Andrea watching over us, I had emerged in Punta Almansa, Morocco, a different person. The swim in Gibraltar showed me that life goes on, and I have to continue living!

After Eduardo's death, I went through a long process of grief. His illness left me with deep wounds and I was forced to look at humanity's vulnerable condition up close. That illness had brought out the worst in me (anguish, fear, anger, and wrath) but also the best of me (strength, courage, love, and tenderness). My husband's death brought out my desolation and I felt devastated and angry. It took many months to finally accept that I was angry at life and, at the same time, extremely sad. A deep-rooted sadness that makes you want to cry all day, making you stare at a fixed point with your head down and feel like the words are stuck in your throat without being able to express what you are feeling. As much as I tried not to feel it, it was constantly there, breaking you down and tearing you apart; nevertheless, it allows you to continue moving forward even if it's against your will.

I couldn't allow myself for pain to stop me or to be stuck in the pain I was feeling because I had to continue working and remain strong for my kids. Lalo and Andrea's pain after the loss of their father is, to this day, what hurts me the most. I understood that this pain would be with them forever and that I couldn't change that. It was hard to understand, but I finally accepted it and realized that the only thing I could do was give them my unconditional love and unconditional support.

The "post-hurricane" process, as we called it back then, after Eduardo's death, was complicated and painful. I had originally thought that the most difficult moment would be the actual death, but in reality, it wasn't so. The most painful and complex moments were afterward in a period I called "the devastation."

It was during this time that we began picking up pieces of pain and grief for us to be able to move forward. It wasn't easy, and it took much longer than we had all anticipated.

"We continued swimming. After a few strokes, I heard Nora yelling: "Mariel, shark!"

She thought I hadn't heard her and she yelled even louder: "Mariel, there's a shark right beneath us!" In that instant, my entire life flashed before my eyes."

Kaiwi Channel, Pacific Ocean, July 2017.

CHAPTER 8
KAIWI CHANNEL

We didn't know how to live in confinement during the pandemic! My mother would call every day and tell me how frustrated she was being unable to go out and carry out her daily routines. My kids began to feel desperate; they couldn't see their friends or go out to do their daily activities and they were always irritable and grumpy. My sister would send us messages telling me how anxious she felt and how scared she was at the thought of her or my nephews—Samuel and Gabriel—getting the virus. They were also fed up with being locked up in their home apartment. My brother-in-law, Enrique, needed to go to work, and every day he came home, he would be incredible fearful at the thought of getting sick or spreading the virus to his family. My aunt didn't even want to talk on the phone because she feared getting sick! These situations didn't only happen to my family; they were happening to everyone all over the world. This pandemic had put everybody on guard as if a shark was circling around its next prey. As I thought of this image, I recalled when I crossed the Kaiwi or Molokai Channel…

Nora and I would swim together in tandem formation. That is, both of us would swim keeping up the same pace. When we began swimming at 6:15 pm on the afternoon of July 9th, 2017, we both knew that it would be a long journey. We were to begin at sunset and continue swimming in the dark. This swim would take all night.

We flew from Oahu Island to Molokai that same morning. It only took about twenty minutes, and during the flight, we flew over the blue waters we would be swimming that evening. How relative the concept of distance can be - at that moment, it took us only a few minutes to cover the same distance and we would take about twelve hours to swim across.

When we landed in Molokai, we breathed a different air. This air filled our lungs with excitement and uncertainty at the same time. We left the small airport and many people approached us offering different hotel accommodations around the island. They gave us strange looks when we told them we wouldn't need a place to stay because we would swim back to Oahu that evening. They responded, "Good luck and have a good swim."

A taxi drove us to the starting point. We waited around five hours until our escort boat showed up. I began to get nervous. I tried to enjoy the beach and the view of the ocean, the trees all around, and the sound of the wind and the waves, but I was not able to relax. I was overwhelmed by the many thoughts and emotions facing this challenge.

Tried as I might, I couldn't find a sense of calm, so I decided to walk around until finally, I sat under a tree to listen to the sound of the ocean. I tried meditation to fill myself with energy and stay centered and at peace.

The tree not only gave me shade, but it also had a very special effect on me. Its trunk reminded me of the strength I would need to swim the forty-two kilometers of sea. Its leaves that formed a canopy from the sun and covered me reminded me of the wonders in nature and the infinite and eternal order of things, of the magic of the sun and moon, and each thing that has its own moment in time. These thoughts helped ground me and filled me with positive energy for what was to come. I took deep breaths, and as I filled my lungs, I nourished my entire being with the different aromas that surrounded me. I could visualize my body swimming, and I could see the bubbles I would blow out with each breath underwater. I saw my hands touching the grass and could feel the dampness. As I opened my eyes, I was filled by a bright light that had filtered through the tree's branches.

While I was waiting, I also thought about my children. Lalo and Andrea who had stayed behind in Oahu. Both were probably enjoying a perfect day at the beach but would be attentive to any news about my swim. I thought back to when they were babies, their tiny hands and first steps, chubby cheeks, and bright eyes, curious about their new world discoveries.

Laying there under the shade of that tree, I reflected on life and my existence. I was aware that life passes by quickly without us realizing it until years pass by and we are able to look back on our life's journey. Little by little, I was able to regain my sense of calm. A few hours later, I saw our escort boat approaching from a distance. I knew that we were a few minutes from our Kaiwi swim in the imposing Pacific Ocean!

Nora and I got ready for the challenge under the shade of that tree. We were very excited to share this experience. If we were able to complete the swim, we would be the first Mexican women to accomplish this challenge. Arleen and Gela, our two dear friends and fellow swimmers, would be part of our support crew for this journey, and they helped us get ready for the swim.

The moments right before a swim are filled with anxiety, excitement and uncertainty. You never know what to expect and can only hope the conditions will be good. As soon as I was ready, I tried to visualize the path to Oahu. I was wary about the fact that it would take all night. I knew that the mystery of life is always interwoven in the darkness and so I decided to trust that everything would be alright.

At the water's edge on the beach, I took a deep breath and filled myself with sunlight, trying to hold on to those afternoon rays to take with me during the swim. As I heard the horn from the escort boat, Nora and I ran to the water and started swimming.

We swam very fast those first meters, flying through the water as we left the beach behind. The drops of water that splashed around us left small rainbows that filled us with color. The sun slowly began to set, turning the once blue ocean into a black one. The bubbles were barely visible and we could almost see the reddish light from the kayak that was guiding our route. The escort boat was about 400 meters ahead and, because of the high surf, we would lose sight of it from moment to moment. The sky had a faint amber glow as it illuminated the clouds above, and a few moments into the swim, the moon began to rise. The white moon was our companion during the night, casting a light on the crests of the waves and giving the sea a silver glow that marked our path.

During the first three or four hours, our swim was uneventful. However, at a certain moment, as I swam between Nora and the kayak, I couldn't focus on a fixed point of reference, and I began to feel dizzy. Everything was moving. When I tried to look at the boat, I could see a blinking light that also moved. Even the moon in its orbit had shifted.

I felt extremely dizzy but never stopped swimming. I kept searching for a point of reference to hang on to as a means to reduce my discomfort. Every half an hour, we would approach the boat to hydrate. I mentioned that I wasn't feeling well at one of those stops. I resisted saying that I was feeling nauseous for fear that the crew would think I wasn't in any condition to continue swimming, but as soon as I said it, I felt better. Sometimes it helps to ask for help, even though it might be scary to do so, as if it were a sign of weakness to ask for assistance. On the next stop, they mixed a nausea medication in my drink and a few minutes later the dizziness went away and I felt a lot better.

Because of the high surf, Nora and I often lost sight of the boat ahead of us. On one occasion, I saw two lights instead of one—one much brighter than the other. I asked the kayaker what that light was, and he told me that it was the Oahu lighthouse, which was in the direction we were heading.

My memories brought me back to an evening when I was about five or six years old. I was sitting on a terrace at my grandparents' house, watching the ocean in Acapulco. I recall seeing a light that would appear and disappear in the distance. I couldn't make sense of it because I thought all the lights around us didn't appear and disappeared. "Why does this happen to that light in particular?" I asked dad. "It's the lighthouse that guides the ships that come into the harbor," he answered. I had never even heard of the word "lighthouse," much less seen one. During daylight, it was impossible to see it from the place we were staying.

I needed to see the lighthouse from Oahu as a reminder that it was guiding my path. I also thought of my dad, who had been my personal lighthouse, illuminating my journey by example with his peaceful disposition, patience, and smile. In the lower light, I also saw my mother, a woman filled with joy, enthusiasm, and a passion for life as she taught me about the world. I felt a sense of contentment thinking about my parents; both of them was the light guiding me in this journey.

These thoughts brought a smile to my face. It was such an authentic feeling that nothing could wipe it away. In fact, at that precise moment, a jellyfish stung my mouth, and I felt the pain in my tongue and teeth. I screamed with pain, "Oh, those jellyfish!"

That night, the Oahu lighthouse helped me find my point of reference which also helped reduce my nausea. It was the light I needed to see and it was the light that clearly marked where I was heading. It was my guiding light in the distance. The light that brings ships to safety illuminated my mind and shed light on what was important as I traveled life's path.

We had been swimming for twelve hours! I didn't know how long we were left to get to our destination, but I felt fortunate that we had gotten this far, overcoming the dark, the surf, the nausea, the wind, and even the jellyfish. The day broke in the most beautiful way possible: it was a sunrise with a full moon! The ocean was filled with the clarity of the morning light and took on a bluish hue. We were swimming in water that was transparent, clear, and blue!

When we stopped to hydrate, I asked for some sweet peaches. I thought the sweetness would help alleviate the sting on my tongue because of the salt water and the jellyfish. They tossed me a small bag full of peaches, and I savored them with my eyes closed. I could still taste them on my tongue for the following moments before I continued swimming. "Here we come, Oahu," I thought. "We are close, and the sun is about to come out on the horizon." I felt happy that everything was working out as planned.

At that exact moment, I heard Nora yell: "Mariel, shark!" "What? Where? Oh, please, no!" I moved my head around, trying to see the fin above the water. "It's under us!" yelled

Nora. I thought: "Breakfast!"

I wanted to be able to walk on water and run away. The only thing I could do was stay right there next to Nora. We were floating close to the kayak and searching underwater, so scared without knowing what to do…and my entire life flashed before my eyes!

Meanwhile, Mike, the kayaker, kept urging us to continue swimming. We had to move forward. I thought, "How can we keep swimming with a shark under us?" I felt scared and, while floating, tried to remain calm. I put my head underwater to see if the shark was there, hoping I wouldn't see it and praying it was gone. Mike tried to calm us down: "It was probably just curious." I let out a quick laugh. "It was curious…wow, what a fright its curiosity gave us!"

Mike insisted we continue swimming and told us it was important to overcome our fears to move forward. He said, "To swim the Kaiwi Channel, you need to overcome many fears. The sharks are only one of them." He was so right! That shark didn't bother us again. With every stroke, I felt us getting closer to the coast, and I was filled with the confidence to continue, even though I kept a lookout to see if the shark would come back.

We had been swimming for fourteen hours when my eyes suddenly filled with all the colors in the world. It was a kaleidoscope of colors and shapes. Thousands of fish were swimming under us quickly, leaving an aquatic rainbow that filled me with joy! It was crazy to see the amount of fish gliding under us from side to side.

We were swimming over a coral reef! When I took a breath and looked into the distance, I saw that the coast was near. I only wanted to reach the beach, walk out of the ocean, and hug my children. I wanted to hold them in a strong embrace that would last us for eternity.

Swimming the Kaiwi Channel, the 42 kilometers from the Island of Molokai to Oahu, took us fourteen hours and twenty-eight minutes. It was a journey of learning and, above all, about defeating deep-rooted fears.

In my experience, when we swim through life we face many of our fears, not only the fear of sharks but those other "imaginary sharks" we all face when we look in the mirror. Those are the dangerous ones; they make you believe you are not capable or worthy of accomplishing your dreams, they tell you, "You better quit" or "You don't deserve this." You must eradicate those imaginary sharks to move forward and keep on swimming through life!

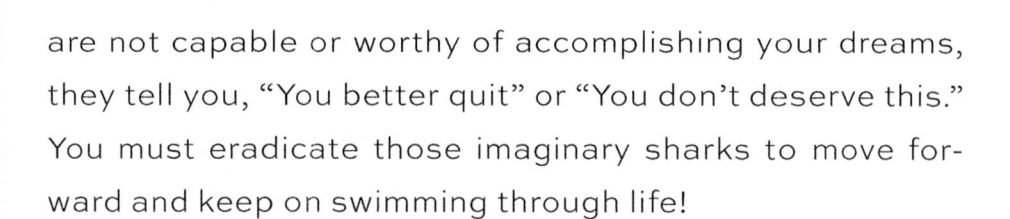

"I was confronted by: my anxiety, my anger, my wrath, frustration, and my sadness.

Facing my darkest self has helped me be courageous, and also understand, comprehend, forgive and love myself more."

Tsugaru Strait, Japan, July 2018.

CHAPTER 9
TSUGARU STRAIT

It was mid-April 2020, and COVID-19 was rampant! The situation we were living in in Mexico City was alarming. The days went by and more people were getting sick. Hospitals and health centers were overbooked and lacked the necessary ventilators to treat critical patients. They didn't have the required protective gear for their personnel. Doctors and health care professionals urged the population to stay at home to avoid exposure, confirming that they were also scared for their own personal well-being. I heard a doctor mention that the nursing staff at the hospital was at a greater risk than doctors themselves and that comment touched a nerve with both me and mom. Mom, a nurse herself, immediately called me and told me that we needed to do "something" to support her colleagues who were exposing themselves to the virus while caring for their sick patients. I had no idea how we could help until it suddenly came to me.

I decided to offer online courses and use the money to purchase protective gear for the nursing staff in the different public hospitals that had been designated COVID centers.

I explained my idea to mother, but she understood nothing about "online workshops" and "virtual assistants." Regardless, she urged me to do it and said, "Make sure you help all the nurses you can because they need us."

And so I did. I advertised an "In the Midst of the Storm, Your Heart at Peace" workshop through social media. To my surprise, many people signed up and paid the fee. The workshop was streamed via Zoom and was tailored in a way where I could share my experiences. The main idea was to share my many experiences during many of my swims with real-life situations we have all faced. I wanted to provide a platform where we could all share our emotions. I shared with the audience tools that have helped me to manage my feelings in a healthy way.

I conducted four workshops in total, which allowed us to buy many basic needs products such as food, hygiene products, protection gear, masks, and protection suits, among others. It was a blessing to be able to personally distribute the goods to the nursing staff in the following hospitals: Instituto Nacional de Enfermedades Respiratorias (INER), Instituto Nacional de Neurología, which became a COVID center, Instituto Nacional de Cardiología, and the Hospital

General 20 de Noviembre, all of which are in Mexico City.

Every time I visited any of these health centers, I would take the necessary precautions. Each delivered donation kit had all the basic needs for hygiene, food, and protection gear, but also lots of love since we had included short notes with messages thanking the staff for their service.

I was able to thank each participant personally through my social media for being a part of the workshop, "In the Midst of the Storm, Your Heart at Peace," and that reminded me of the time I crossed the Tsugaru Channel in Japan. My first attempt was in September 2016, and the second was two years later.

At the end of September 2016, I traveled to Cape Tappi, Japan, to swim the Tsugaru Strait. I was instantly captivated by the silence of the place and its majestic view from the Tsugaru lighthouse. Every day, I would hike to a nearby beach where I would swim and train. I would alternate between swimming in the Sea of Japan or the Pacific Ocean each day. I spent five days freely enjoying the beauty that this place had to offer.

The day before the swim, I met with Captain Mizushima to get to know him and understand the journey's details. He invited us to his home, along with Mr. Yusuke, who would be the translator and part of the technical crew. The Captain spoke formally, and Yusuke translated his words. At first, he was full of greetings and formalities; however, when the translator said that the weather would be unstable (to put it lightly), I turned to look at the television that was showing satellite images. I saw that the weather wasn't unstable, but in fact it was terrible! I don't speak Japanese, but the satellite images were clear and overwhelming. I was ultimately against it and told him so, but the Captain said, "My destiny was to swim the following day!" Destiny? What destiny?

I wanted to scream but I held it tight in my throat and I did not want to make a sound. I didn't show my frustration or anger either; I couldn't understand why we couldn't just simply wait a few days for the weather to improve.

I left the meeting with an uneasy feeling. I thought the weather would improve that night so I went to bed trying to get as much rest as possible. I woke up at midnight because of a strange noise that seemed to be coming from inside the closet. I got up to check making sure that everything was ok. I saw the hangers crashing into each other. The wind coming from the open window was causing them to move so I went to close it. I saw it was beginning to rain. I went back to bed hoping it would stop in a few hours and the wind would subside.

As much as I tried, I wasn't able to fall back asleep. I felt uneasy, and when my alarm went off at two in the morning, I noticed the wind had picked up, and the rain was pouring down heavy. These were the worst conditions for an open-water swim!

When we left the hotel, it was dark and rainy and the winds were strong. Even so, we went to the docks. The Captain was busy preparing everything and didn't even greet us when we arrived. The translator asked Gela, Nora, and me to prepare everything so we could make it to the starting point as soon as possible. We moved quickly, and the boat was set to go at three in the morning.

The waters were very choppy when we left the docks and the protected zone. Between the high surf and the rain, we had absolutely no visibility and the motion was intense.

The translator asked us to find refuge in a small cabin that measured about one meter by a meter and a half (3 ft by 5 ft), where the gasoline was stored. A few minutes inside that cabin, the three of us were pale, nauseous and feeling very scared. We saw the Captain shout something to the translator through the tiny window, but we couldn't understand what they were saying. We were sitting side by side on the ground but kept crashing into each other with the boat's irregular and strong motion. We felt the boat turn around towards the docks a few minutes later. Navigating in these conditions was impossible, much less swimming in them!

We came back to the departure spot, and the Captain decided it was best to wait until sunrise. We set sail again right before the sun came out, but the weather hadn't changed a bit; the wind, surf, and tide were still strong. It was raining but with much less intensity than before. I still hoped that the weather conditions would begin improving soon.

Once we arrived at the starting point, the sky was overcast and gray, it was windy, and the waves were huge. Even so, the Captain gave the order for me to jump in the water to begin swimming. I followed his command trusting that he knew what he was doing and that the conditions would improve soon, otherwise he wouldn't have instructed me to jump in.

As I began swimming, I felt as if I was climbing up each giant wave that came my way. I was being tossed around by the waves and had to swim underwater to move forward. The wind picked up as I kept swimming making it very difficult to make any progress. The storm was picking up speed and, at the same time, causing inner turmoil of feelings within me. I felt frustrated, angry, and extremely disappointed at what was happening. After four hours and thirty-six minutes of swimming, I heard the whistle from the escort boat telling me to stop swimming and that my attempt to cross Tsugaru Strait was now cancelled. The explanation was simple: the weather had gotten worse putting everybody at risk. I was being forced to get out of the water and as I heard them speak, I was not able to process the fact that I would not be able to continue my swim. I did not want to stop, even if the storm became rampant. I shouted back at them, "This isn't the first time that I have swum in the midst of a storm. I want to keep going!" But their response once again was for me stop swimming. "Get out of the water at once!" I remained in the water, trying to get rid of all the negative feelings and anger I was feeling inside me. I recalled the words from the day before, "my destiny," and felt even more turmoil and frustration. I continued swimming for a few minutes in those terrible conditions realizing that the fury of storm and the waves was a reflection of what I was feeling inside. And, suddenly, my head was deep underwater and I experienced something unexpectedly amazing: at the bottom of the sea the waters were calm.

I felt exhausted after almost five hours of swimming in those tumultuous waters. The wind had caused huge surf and I had never been tossed around so much as it happened in that storm. The calm seas from the previous days had become turbulent, violent, and an angry ocean, and with every stroke that I swam, it would send huge waves in my direction. The ocean reacted to the strong winds, resulting in complicated waves. However strong was the wind, the waves, and the surf, it never impacted the serenity of the deep ocean waters. Marine life remained calm and continued in its own serene rhythm. As I realized this, all the anger, frustration, and storm of emotions that had been brewing within me completely disappeared and I also regained a sense of calm.

Almost immediately, I stopped swimming and boarded the boat. Nature follows its own path and even though I prayed for the winds to stop and the clouds to disappear, I swam in turbulent conditions which the Captain coined as "my destiny." That day, as I swam in the middle of the storm, I discovered the heart of the ocean: a calm and serene heart which I made my own.

Two years after that experience, in July 2018, I came back to Japan. As we flew across the Pacific Ocean on our way to Tokyo, Andrea slept beside me on the plane. When I saw her curled up sleeping, I thought what a privilege it was to have her accompany me. She didn't think twice about coming along when I suggested to her to join me in this trip. In fact, at one point, I had doubts whether she would be coming or not, but that was quickly settled when she said, "I'm ready to come with you and be part of your support team during the crossing of Tsugaru!"

Andrea is always a step ahead. She doesn't see obstacles; each challenge is met with enthusiasm and self-confidence. She wasn't swimming, but she would support me during the journey in the Strait of Tsugaru.

Andrea was still asleep when the Captain announced that we had begun our descent. I woke her up to tell her we were about to land, and enthusiastically, she said, "Mom, we are almost in Japan; we haven't been this far ever!" We hadn't traveled this far before, and I thought that we would surely go further still together.

An hour later, we landed in the Narita International Airport. It took us fourteen hours to get there, but it went by quickly as I had spent much of the flight recalling many pleasant memories. From then on, things happened rather quickly. We went through customs, got our luggage, exchanged some money, bought a cell phone chip, and got bus tickets that would take us to Haneda airport to catch our next flight to Aomori—the northernmost city on Japan's main island.

In Aomori, we transferred to Cape Tappi, a small settlement in the Tsugaru Strait, between the Sea of Japan and the Pacific Ocean, in front of the Island of Hokkaido.

The car ride to Tappi takes about an hour and a half long (approximately 100 kilometers away) and is a beautiful scenic route. As you get closer to Tappi, all civilization is left behind and you are in between the forest and the sea. The road follows the coast until you reach Cape Tappi. Once we finally got to the Hotel Tappi, we were welcomed by a strong wind. The wind lifted us off the ground and was strong enough to toss us around. We couldn't stand still, and everything was moving around us. It seemed to me that history was repeating itself, and I panicked! Andrea saw the look on my face and understood immediately what was going through my mind. At that moment, we looked at each other and cracked up laughing. We had to wait a few days anyway, and I decided not to think too much about it and simply enjoy dinner and rest as much as possible. The next day, the wind subsided and it had surely sent out a message that Andrea and I had arrived to Cape Tappi! We had made it to our destination: Cape Tappi in Japan!

The days we spent in Tappi while we waited for the crossing were wonderful. Every day, Andrea would come with me to swim, and after the training session, we would walk around and discover beautiful places in the mountains and the ocean. Breakfast and dinner were also moments of discovery because the hotel only served local food and traditional dishes. We ate many different types of algae, tasting "green" with flavors from the sea, along with shell fish—some of which were still alive! And fish prepared in traditional Japanese recipes. Andrea's eyes would pop out every time she saw the different dishes, but she was always willing to try new things. Some things were not to her liking, but she discovered many others she would love.

Every day, we spent time on the "Onsen," a traditional Japanese bath. We enjoyed the thermal waters that relaxed us and allowed us to spend quality time together as mother and daughter.

On our fourth day, Nora arrived. She came with her mother, Dora, and her son, Max. We would swim the Strait in tandem —it would be registered individually, but we would swim together. We would swim the same distance and at the same pace, just like we had done in the Molokai Channel.

After a few days, Captain Mizushima, whom we already knew, asked us to be at the dock at 2:00 am the following day to begin the adventure. That afternoon, I explained to Andrea what she would have to do as part of the support team. She would have to prepare my hydration drink every half an hour, count my strokes every fifteen minutes, and post my progress on social media. I also explained what she should do and how she should react in case of an emergency. When I got to the emergency part, she took notes, was taking matters seriously, but went on to tell me, "Nothing's going to happen; just swim quickly!"

Once everything we needed was ready, Andrea fell asleep quickly, but I couldn't sleep a wink. What a difficult situation! Andrea, at seventeen, would be responsible for her mother during the entire swim and would have to make decisions that other young people her age would never have to face. On the other hand, I knew that Max, also seventeen, would be doing the same for Nora, the only difference being that Dora, his grandmother, would also be on board. Andrea would be by herself. I found some sense of peace that Yusuke, the translator, spoke English well and offered to help Andrea during the entire journey. As I thought about all these details, the hours passed, and finally, the alarm went off at one in the morning. When we reached the docks at two in the morning, a light rain started to fall and my thoughts were filled with a rainstorm of uncertainty. Captain Mizushima asked us to get closer to the boat but didn't let us board yet. He sat down and showed us some images on his iPad as he explained something to us. He talked quickly and non-stop. We listened in silence without understanding a single word he was saying. When he finished talking, the translator told us the Captain was advising us to return to our hotel to rest until the next day because the weather conditions would be much better. He went on to say that we would have to be at the docks at midnight so we could start the swim no later than one in the morning. Captain Mizushima was serious when he said that he expected it to be a very good day for our crossing.

The following day, we began swimming at one in the morning. It was completely dark with a faint fog was floating up in the air. The water temperature was around 15ºC (59ºF), and the ocean was peaceful, very peaceful. As I swam, I glided easily, and without much effort and after about an hour and a half, when we stopped to hydrate, Andrea told us we were doing well and to continue swimming fast. We were swimming at a good pace, but also, in the words of Mizushima, we were having a good night swimming with the tide in our favor.

We swam in total darkness for five hours. The only light was from the boat that was guiding our path through the Strait of Tsugaru towards Hakodate. At dawn, it began raining and the fog became denser; however, the waters remained calm without any waves whatsoever. We were gliding on a silky, liquid surface. After six hours, we still couldn't see the coast, but when we stopped to hydrate, the message was clear, "You are close to getting there; you can't see the coastline because of the fog, but if you keep swimming at this pace, you will make record time."

"Mom, swim faster! Mom, faster! You are almost there! Mom, keep going; it's almost over, and you'll make it in record time!" Andrea kept us going with her words of encouragement.

I couldn't believe it. It was like swimming in the middle of a cloud. I couldn't see past the boat, and it was difficult to picture that we were so close to the shore. We kept swimming, and a few minutes later, we heard the whistle from the boat. When we stopped to get our instructions, they passed us the Mexican flag, and it was at that precise moment the wind picked up and the fog cleared. I saw that we were only 300 – 500 meters from reaching Hakodate. We swam those last few meters as fast as we could, reaching the rocks in the midst of a downpour. We were able to complete the swim of the Strait of Tsugaru in 6 hours and 20 minutes. As we climbed out of the water onto the rocks, we both held the flag from Mexico, posed for a picture together, and a seagull, who wanted to be a part of our feat, landed next to us.

We climbed aboard and hugged. On the way back to Cape Tappi, we celebrated with Andrea, Max, Dora, and Captain Mizushima, along with his support crew—Yusuke and Mr. Moriya, the representative of the Strait of Tsugaru Swim Association. The seagull that had joined us in our picture surely also wanted to celebrate and invited her friends to do so since a flock of them flew above us to Tappi. They circled our boat above as if to congratulate us for the swim.

When we reached the port, the seagulls flew back to their nests, and it began raining again. The seagulls and the rain were an important part of this challenge and the celebration.

Back in our hotel room, I embraced Andrea wholeheartedly. As I held her tightly, I felt tears fall down my face with a sense of pride and admiration at how she had managed during the entire swim. I thanked her for her commitment, support, and love. I hugged her even more tightly and told her: "You have the words of a prophet. I swam fast, and the entire time, it was you who pushed me to do it and keep up the pace. We made it together and will continue to do so in the future!"

The crossing of the Strait of Tsugaru on July 1st, 2018, was done in an extraordinary record time of 6 hours, 20 minutes and 52 seconds. This record has been recognized by the World of Open Water Swimming Association and by Guinness World Records.

I received the Guinness World Record certificate almost two years later, feeling very satisfied and accomplished. I recalled the magic of the ocean in Tsugaru and the change in tide. Well, as they say... "the tides always change!"

"I swim the last strokes, having been in the water for a little over seventeen minutes in 6°C temperatures, and as I get out of the water, I see my reflection in the car's windshield.

My skin looks green, almost purple, and is wrinkled; the goggles left their mark around my eyes, leaving pronounced wrinkles, and my lips are swollen because of the cold. I have two red marks around my neck that look raw and about to bleed because of the bathing suit chafing my skin as I swam, but despite all of this I look at my reflection and smile!"

Nevado de Toluca's crater, Mexico, 2007.

CHAPTER 10
INTO COLD WATER

The months passed by with growing uncertainty. What we had thought would only last a few weeks kept on going for a month and a half already, and more and more people were getting sick with COVID-19. There weren't any vaccines to reduce the risk, and the medical treatment was still not accurate: some people got better and recovered, but many got complications and died.

I decided to take care of myself and my family in every way possible, but as time passed I felt a deep need to swim again. Each day that I stayed away from the water, ironically, felt as if I was drowning. So, I began searching for a way to resume swimming without putting anyone at risk. I found an outdoor pool that no one was using and I would take advantage of that situation to swim a few kilometers three times a week.

In one occasion, I got back home after training only to realize that we were out of gas. The service had been irregular during the past three months. I had no choice but to take a cold shower. While I was in the shower I recalled the time

I swam in the Laguna del Sol in Toluca. This lagoon was formed in the crater of an extinct volcano called Nevado de Toluca, near Mexico City. It is at 4,000 meters (12,000 ft) above sea level and has a diameter of around 400 meters. That was when I began getting used to cold-freezing water temperatures that would help my mind and body for the upcoming swim of the English Channel and many more swims in water temperatures below 15ºC (59ºF) that followed.

The first time I swam in the volcano, in April 2007, it was an overcast morning with a light freezing rain. The water temperature in the lagoon was around 6ºC (43ºF). The process of getting into the water was a slow and complicated process; the moment my feet touched the freezing water they started to hurt. I felt an intense shot of pain, but a few seconds later I lost all sensation. The same effect happened to my legs—I felt a sharp pain that reached my bones, but a few seconds later, it disappeared and I lost all sensibility. I remained still for a few minutes, almost paralyzed- I couldn't make myself keep going, but I didn't want to give up either. Finally, I went in a little deeper, and when the water reached my waist, I had the feeling that my body was split in half: the bottom part of my body didn't want to keep going and the upper part urging me to continue moving forward. I knew I would have to jump in and begin swimming. Again, I remained with the sensation that my body had two parts and all of a sudden I yelled from the top of my lungs, "I can do this!" and I put my head underwater. That moment became imprinted in my mind...the pain in my chest and face was so intense that it felt like someone was squeezing my lungs and even with goggles on, my eyes hurt! I was having trouble breathing, felt like my lungs couldn't expand, and I got scared. It took a great effort, but I calmed down allowing the oxygen, which was already scarce at four thousand meters above sea level, to fill in my lungs. I began moving my arms quickly, noting that they felt so heavy and required maximum effort. My jaw became stiff and I couldn't close my mouth. Every time I put my face in the water, I felt an electric charge of sensibility on my teeth. During those seventeen minutes, my entire will and energy were consumed.

It took me a long time to get out of the water. I felt lethargic and as much as I tried to move quickly my body was slow to respond. I began shaking uncontrollably; I couldn't talk and had lost all feeling in my hands and feet. My friend and fellow swimmer, Julie, had come with me from ashore that day to support me. She helped dry me and climb into the car where she had turned the heater on. Once inside, she helped me change into dry and warm clothes. The trembling lasted almost an hour, and I was able to speak about half an hour later. On our way back to Mexico City, I sipped warm ginger tea with lemon which helped me get warm again.

The cold hurts and the pain is not easy to manage; however, you get used to it. Each time I take a cold shower, I remember that day in the Nevado de Toluca, and I say, "The water is not so cold; enjoy it!"

I called the process of getting used to cold waters "The Path of Cold"—and just as any other path in life, one must start at the beginning and take it one step at a time.

I also began this path as part of my training to get ready for the North Channel between Northern Ireland and Scotland. The water temperatures there would be around 12ºC and 13ºC (54ºF - 55ºF). For me, it's very cold!

This path should be traveled with someone, or else it becomes very solitary. Any path, no matter where it takes you, is easier taken in the company of someone else. The people that love you help you move along the way, step by step. They help by giving you strength and motivate you to continue moving forward, whether they are your children, family, siblings, parents, or even friends. In my case, the love of Lalo and Andrea helped me conquer "The Path of Cold" as I felt the warmth of their ongoing support.

Bathing in cold water was just the first step in preparation for the swim in the San Francisco Bay, which, in turn, would also be a training exercise for the swim I would complete in the North Channel.

"It's cold, I can feel it on my face, hands and neck...I breathe in and the freezing air fills my body.

My nose is red and my eyes are watering... When the tide reaches my feet, my toes automatically shrink trying not to feel. I put on my goggles to protect my eyes, and I take a step forward..."

San Francisco Bay, California, January 2018

CHAPTER 11
NEXT STOP, THE NORTH CHANNEL

A few months later, it was finally time to travel to San Francisco. I recall the exact moment vividly: very cold, standing by at the edge of the water, waiting for the tides to reach my feet, and finally taking a step into the water to begin swimming... I hadn't even started and I was already freezing!

As soon as the water reached my toes, I felt an electric current move up my entire body. I took a deep breath, trying to relax through the pain. Slowly, I stepped forward as each centimeter of water moved up to cover my body. My mind kept telling me, "Stop and get out of the water!" but I kept on going. When the water reached my hips, I splashed water on my arms and face and said, "It's now or never!" I jumped in and began swimming. I felt a sharp pain in my face underwater and I thought to myself, "Mariel, you know this was going to happen; it always does with the first dive. It feels like it is squeezing you and taking your breath away. Relax and keep going."

I kept saying to myself: "Mariel, relax, keep calm, one stroke at a time."

When you swim in cold waters, with temperatures under 14°C or 15°C (57°F - 59°F), your lungs contract, and it feels like they can't fill up with oxygen. The cold seems to paralyze your body. After a few strokes, your body feels heavy, and it takes a tremendous amount of effort to move your arms. Your face feels cramped and your jaw clamps. When the water enters your ear canal, it also freezes your brain. A few minutes later, your body feels like there are a thousands needles pinching you and they burn. It is a strange sensation that lasts a second, and once it is gone, the cold remains and takes over every part of your body. I recalled looking at my watch and noticed that I had only been swimming for ten minutes! **TEN MINUTES!!!**

I was suffering and, yet, I had already swum for ten minutes in 10°C (50°F) water at the Aquatic Park in San Francisco Bay, California. I decided to continue for a little while longer without knowing how long I would last, but I kept swimming, trying not to think of the cold. I kept trying to relax my mind, breathing deeply with each inhalation and every exhale, trying my best to enjoy the cold waters. I said to myself, "Enjoy it!" and my next thought was, "I can't believe I am telling myself to enjoy this torture; I must be losing my mind!"

As I continued swimming, I opened and closed my purple hands. I wanted to keep up the circulation in my limbs and recover some of the life and warmth that the freezing water drains from our extremities. I also kicked my legs forcefully to generate warmth, but it only resulted in cramps on my feet and calves. I couldn't kick anymore and wasn't able to generate warmth. Lesson learned.

I had to keep swimming to return to the beach where I had jumped in the water, which was about 400 meters away. I hoped not to freeze on my way back. I only thought of getting back so I could take a hot shower. The return wasn't long; it was eternal!

Finally, out of the water, I couldn't stop the tears of frustration. I had only been able to swim in these waters for 45 minutes. How would I register and prove the eight hour swim in 12°C–13°C (54°F - 56°F) temperatures required by the Swim Association of the North Channel? This was an obligatory requirement by the association to approve the swim of the North Channel. At that moment, I felt a surge of freezing wind enter the bay from the Golden Gate bridge and hit me straight on my back. It shook and froze me as a reminder that I needed to take this one step at a time and keep calm.

The freezing wind that shook me took all my doubts away and gave me the certainty that I needed to keep training!

I knew that the "The Path of Cold" would be difficult but not impossible. So, it was necessary to keep on going, one step at a time. But at that moment, I needed to rush to a hot shower, which felt my soul returning to my body.

At the end of that week, between Friday and Sunday, I had already swum almost six hours. Besides my hot showers and sauna, I treated myself to delicious "Clam Chowder" that I shared in the company of Gela, who would travel with me to Ireland for the North Channel swim. Miguel Melendez, a fellow swimmer and friend from Peru who lived in San Francisco, would come along on his kayak during my following training session in the San Francisco Bay. This would be my final training to swim for eight consecutive hours and get the Swim Association of the North Channel's approval for my crossing.

Ever since Eduardo's death almost three years ago, my life and that of my family had changed drastically. My kids and

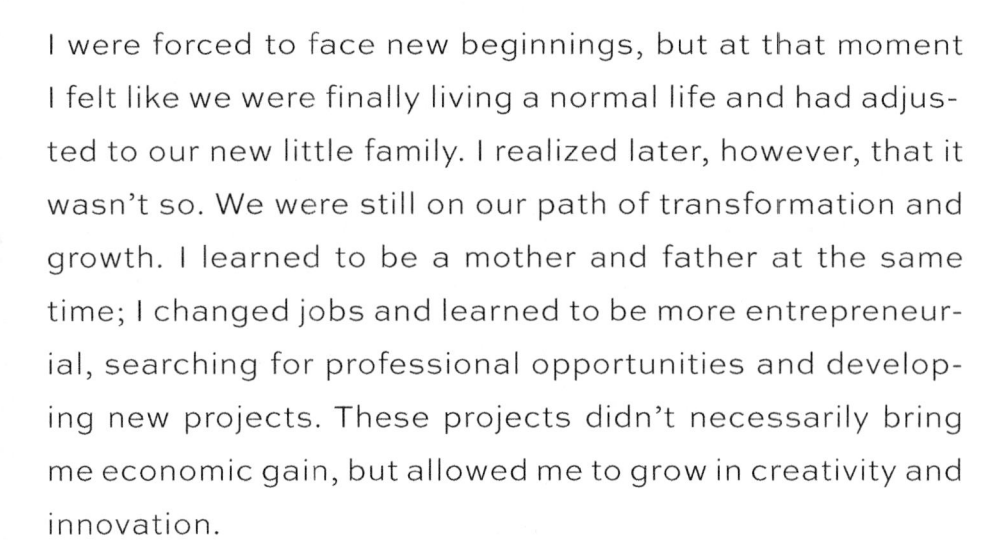

I were forced to face new beginnings, but at that moment I felt like we were finally living a normal life and had adjusted to our new little family. I realized later, however, that it wasn't so. We were still on our path of transformation and growth. I learned to be a mother and father at the same time; I changed jobs and learned to be more entrepreneurial, searching for professional opportunities and developing new projects. These projects didn't necessarily bring me economic gain, but allowed me to grow in creativity and innovation.

I also began a process where my swimming became more intimate and personal. It allowed me to revisit my feelings, emotions, and to be able to identify when I felt sadness, anxiety, fear, nostalgia, anger, frustration, and disappointment. Facing each of these feelings allowed me to deal openly with them while on my path towards dealing with adversity. I dived head-on into the ocean of these emotions that made me vulnerable which had forced me to heal and move on. Just as swimming in open waters leaves marks on your skin, sunburns, ulcers, stomach discomfort, muscle pain, and the swelling of your eyes and tongue, swimming in the ocean of emotions is much more painful and requires significantly more empathy, understanding, and acceptance, but above all, self-love on the path to forgiveness. I learned to find extra hours in the day. I found that the hours before dawn, those moments in between sleep and daybreak, between lucidity and sunrise, these are hidden moments where one can cry over everything, especially over the sadness I felt witnessing my children's grief. Being part and watching their anguish and emotional storms. I share this with others who have seen their children's heartbreak for any reason because when we see our children suffer and lost, we hurt as well. And so, crying at dawn helps us let go.

It is a silent cry in the remaining darkness of night. Where you pray for them, with all your faith, as a way to hug them at a distance even though you don't fully understand what they are going through. It is my way of absorbing their difficulties and alleviating their pain or suffering for whatever reason. It is like a humble wish so that when the sun rises they will be bathed in light and their hearts will feel lighter and at peace.

Back in Mexico City, I continue searching for a swimming pool close to home. I wanted to find one that wasn't heated so that I could continue training in cold waters with temperatures under 18ºC (64ºF). I found one at a club next to my building. It was an outdoor pool twenty-five meters long, and management had decided not to heat it because of its high cost. They decided to keep the water clean and the pool in good condition while the members decided what to do about the water temperature. Some wanted to fill it up and convert it into a garden, so while they made their final decision I was allowed to use it, which was a great for me!

I met "the curious" at that pool. Every afternoon or during the weekends, the curious would come to visit. This made me very happy. The first curious were children. They would show up in the afternoon, coming in pairs or with friends who wanted to see firsthand who was swimming in the freezing pool. They weren't allowed to swim in the pool or get too close. Not even the adults swam in this pool. Nevertheless, they saw a woman swimming every day and even after dark, that crazy lady continued swimming in the freezing water. I was a mystery to them; when they got the courage to come closer they would ask questions. "Why do you swim?" "What do you swim for?" "Is the water very cold?" "Aren't you scared of swimming in the dark?" "How many times has a shark bitten you?" "Have you seen dolphins?" "Do you have friends at sea?" Question after question, until they were all answered and they left content knowing that I had quenched their curiosity. Sometimes they weren't happy, for when I was cold my answers would be abrupt. But they knew that they would find me again on another day and ask about the ocean, its secrets, and storms.

The birds that came close to the pool at dusk were the other curious. They came to drink water but also to see me. They would stand at the pool's edge and stay there motionless. Their yellow eyes would follow me from one side to the other with the rhythm of my strokes. Sometimes, there were only a couple, but other times, there were many bordering the pool and watching me swim back and forth. I felt them motivating me to go on. In an instant, one would begin to chirp, and all the others would follow, trying to tell me something or ask just as the children had before. They would fly back to their nests at nightfall, leaving only silence behind. The fireflies would appear at that moment too, illuminating the garden with their magical lights.

I swam so many kilometers in that pool that I cried when they finally began construction to cover it. When I saw the machinery filling it up, I couldn't stop the flow of tears, realizing that the magic of the mornings and sunsets in those cold waters, along with the company of the curious children, birds, and fireflies, was over. That pool is still alive in my memories. I close my eyes and can picture the children with their chatter and laughter. I also see the birds standing along the border of the pool, keeping me company on those cold, rainy afternoons. Guiding me and motivating me to keep swimming. And, of course, the magical lights of the fireflies illuminated my life.

After a few months, I came back to San Francisco to complete my eight-hour training. I remember waking up early when the city was still asleep. I opened my eyes and saw the clock, trying to fall back asleep. I didn't want to think about what I had to face that day, and feeling hypnotized, I closed my eyes and let my mind drift so that I could take advantage of those few moments of sleep.

It was still dark out and I couldn't tell if it would be sunny. It was foggy and dark. However, I felt excited! Even though it might be a cold and very long day, I was looking forward to Miguel's company since he would be on his kayak along side me during the entire swim. Gela would also be there to give me my food and drink rations. When I got to the South End Rowing Club, around 6 am, I greeted Miguel. He told me to start swimming while Gela and he prepared everything they would need. Getting in the water took all of my willpower because it was still dark and very cold. I had been training for many hours in cold waters, which helped me get used to the water quickly. I began swimming, trying to keep up a comfortable pace so that I would make it during the eight hours that were a requisite for the North Channel Swimming Association. I had been swimming a few laps around the Aquatic Park Cove, but Miguel and Gela were nowhere to be seen!

It started to dawn and I realized I was the only one swimming in those waters, except for a couple of sea lions gliding close to the Aquatic Park entrance towards the bay.

The Aquatic Park Cove is a protected zone within the San Francisco Bay. It is about four hundred meters in diameter. The first time I swam there was in 2010 when I participated in the Alcatraz Triathlon. I had been training for the English Channel and Eduardo had invited me on a trip to San Francisco. He had to work on Thursday and Friday and pushed me to participate in the emblematic "Escape from Alcatraz" that would take place that weekend.

I recalled that the ferry took all the participants to the starting point (next to the Island of Alcatraz). Everyone was wearing a wetsuit, including me, since the organizing committee didn't allow me to go without it. At least I was able to find one without sleeves and one that was above the knee since I wanted this experience to be part of my training for the English Channel.

I was shocked to see the other swimmers' faces when they realized the length they would have to swim. I felt excited at the possibility of swimming from Alcatraz toward the coast as if I were a prisoner swimming towards freedom. I had a huge smile on my face when I jumped in and started swimming. I was able to see my fellow swimmers and their scared expressions when they jumped in. However, my smile only lasted while I was swimming. Once it was time to hop on the bike and start the cycling challenge, my face changed to one of terror as I saw all the others pass me by with a smile on their faces. This terror had only begun. At one point, the climb was so difficult that even though I pedaled, I almost fell backward. Further along, I fell off the bike because I went into a sandy ditch. I got up on the bike again and continued on. Then, it was time for the worst part—the marathon portion. I had to run on the beach, and with each step, my feet sunk in the sand, and each leg felt heavier with each stride. I had to climb a set of stairs from the beach up to the road, and I kept sliding down. When I finally made it to the finish line, I rejoiced as if I had indeed been a prisoner in Alcatraz and had gained my freedom!

I kept remembering all of these memories while swimming that early morning and trying to ignore the cold temperatures. After a few minutes, I saw the kayak approach and Miguel asked me if I was ready to swim toward the Golden Gate bridge. "Of course, I am ready!" I answered immediately, with a tremble in my voice because of the cold.

While we shared pizza and fried calamari the previous evening, Miguel explained the training route. We would leave Aquatic Park Cove on our way to the Golden Gate. I would swim this stretch against the current, so it would take me about two to three hours. On our way back, however, I would return with the current, and it would take me about an hour and a half. I would then continue swimming in the protected zone to complete the time necessary for the training session. I fell asleep that night, knowing I would have an excellent training session that would require all my energy.

I continued swimming following the kayak, and once we left the protected zone, I felt the force of the current. I wasn't making much progress, but I felt the company of two female sea lions that kept me company for a few minutes. They probably mistook me for another member of their group. As I got closer to the Golden Gate bridge, I could feel the tide getting stronger. Despite the cold water, I was amazed at the expanse of the ocean in front of me and I kept on swimming. The high surf complicated the swim. One of the waves hit me and I swallowed so much water that it seemed like I had drunk the entire ocean.

I didn't stop because of the cold, the waves, or even the constant doubts in my head. I kept swimming during the eight hours that the session lasted. After eight hours of swimming nonstop, I felt the cold ooze into every cell of my body. I was freezing, feeling the pain in my hands and feet, and having to double my efforts to generate warmth, but the entire time I was aware of my strokes and my breathing, the waves, and the wind. The currents against me made it difficult to move forward, but when the current was in my favor, it helped me flow easily in sync with the beating of my heart.

When I got out of the water, I was cold, but I knew that if nature gave me a good day, I could swim across the North Channel!

"The secrets of the ocean are hidden in each tiny drop of seawater…I begin to swim and feel the cold taking over.

The first strokes are painful, but I know the drill: after a few minutes in the water the body begins to battle the cold and it feels like thousands of needles pricking your skin. This effect helps you during the first half an hour, or better yet, the first twenty minutes…

Later, during the following hours, the only thing my skin will feel is the water that is between 12°C and 13°C."

Dunaghadee, Northern Ireland, August 2018.

CHAPTER 12
THE NORTH CHANNEL

I recall my mother's and Aunt Alejandra's excitement when they told me they would come with me on the trip to Ireland on August 2018 for my crossing of the North Channel. They weren't the only ones excited...if I was able to complete this challenge, it would make me the first latin-american woman to swim from Northern Ireland to Scotland. Swimming the North Channel means a distance of 35 kilometers with water temperatures ranging between 12ºC and 13ºC (54ºF and 55ºF). I knew that to succeed in this challenge, I would have to be strong physically, mentally, and emotionally. In other swims I had enjoyed the journey, but I knew that to swim the North Channel, the cold would seep deep into every fiber of my body and it could put any swimmer in danger. For this not to happen, I would have to rely on positive emotions that would give me with energy needed for me to reach the shore.

During the six days prior to the swim I trained in the Bay of Dunaghadee at least a couple of kilometers each day, trying to get my body used to these cold waters. I recalled the hours I had swum in the San Francisco Bay, fortified my mind with positive thoughts, and filled myself with positive emotions that made me feel good. After my training sessions, the Chunky Dunkers, (swimmers from the area) would wait for me with warm tea and delicious homemade cakes and cookies. It was a treat to train in Dunaghadee! Every afternoon, I would spend time with my mom, walking the path along the ocean and remembering happy moments from my childhood with Aline and dad.

It was still dark on August 20th, 2018, when I jumped in the water. It was 6:00 am, and I felt the first impact of the cold temperature. I felt my lungs deflate and my muscles tense up. I had gone through these reactions in my past trainings so I kept calm, breathed as deep as I could, and swam toward the rocks of the starting point. I was able to stand above the water line, shivering but excited! Full of emotion and expectation about what was about to happen, I heard the boat's horn and the local swimmers' cheers. At that precise moment, I jumped in the water once again and began swimming from Northern Ireland towards Scotland.

I came across the first jellyfish and tried to swim past it. However, a few meters ahead, it was impossible to evade the famous lion's mane jellyfish that stung my arm as I swam past it, inflicting severe pain on me. Even with little or no light, I could see many of these jellyfish up ahead. These jellyfish are commonly found in arctic waters. I knew that they would make this crossing a bit more complicated. I began counting my strokes trying to concentrate, but I kept losing count as I tried to evade the jellyfish. I decided to count them, going from one up to fifty and starting again. They were like flowers in the ocean and this precise image made me feel like I was swimming in a jellyfish garden.

Before I undertook this challenge, I made the conscious decision not to suffer any additional afflictions if at all possible. The cold alone would be the test that would push me to my limit and this is why I established my own personal goal of "The Path of Cold" to get ready and prepare for the North Channel crossing. Even more difficult than the cold would be the thirty-four-kilometer distance that this challenge would entail. I needed a strategy to generate body heat and keep calm so I could swim at a regulated pace. These three factors are fundamental to not fall into hypothermia. It is essential to keep the mind occupied and to keep a steady rhythm while swimming. If any of these fail the entire swim is at risk and I didn't want that to happen.

In the midst of the jellyfish garden, I began recalling memories from my past. Love has always helped me through difficult moments. It fills you with life, makes your heart beat fast, lights up your eyes, warms your soul, and draws a giant smile on your face. That is what it feels like to love: warm, happy, excited, light, and it smells good…like warm bread. I remembered the very first time I hugged my children, their warm bodies next to mine, the excitement of their first words, little hands exploring the world around them, their first steps, their pink cheeks after running or laughing, their merry eyes, their kisses and their unconditional love. Those feelings helped me to swim for many hours; they made me feel warm and kept my mind calm as I swam at a regular pace.

Every time I moved my head to take a breath, I saw Gela and Nora on the boat. Both smiled, and that made me happy and enthusiastic. I was happy to see them. It was cold outside, so they dressed up, even with gloves, but always smiling. Gela prepared my hydrating drink every half an hour, and Nora kept vigilant at all times. After about six hours, I didn't see Nora on the boat, and I thought it was strange. Then I heard a splash. Nora had jumped in to swim by my side for an hour. It is incredible to have company during the swim!

Eight hours had gone by, and during that time, I was able to count more than twenty jellyfish that passed me by, stinging me. Some on my legs, but mostly on my shoulders and arms. Each jellyfish sting provoked an intense burning sensation that would eventually cease because the cold water numbed the sting. I had been stung by other kinds of jellyfish, but this kind of sting hurt the worst and the pain would not completely go away. The jellyfish garden had become a difficult and painful arena.

After swimming for about ten hours, I was finally able to see the coast of Scotland clearly. However, as much as I swam, I couldn't make up for the distance and the cold began taking over me. I was starting to feel desperate! I knew this moment could come. Cold temperatures and the pain from the jellyfish stinging me were finally taking its toll. The sense of desperation grew exponentially in a very short period of time, allowing negative thoughts to make their way into my head. Try as I may to relax and calm down; I was cold and in pain. I hadn't been able to warm myself up and as much as I tried to keep negative thoughts at bay, I found it impossible. I had reached my limit and I exploded. I felt like screaming out of pain, out of my cold, and yelling out my frustrations so that I could find the strength to go on!

In many occasions, frustration and anger have helped me find the strength to continue. Little by little, I was able to let go of those negative feelings and I was able to focus on making progress. The pain began to subside, which was good. I realized that I couldn't really do anything about the cold except to ignore it. I also realized that I was actually beating the strong current and heading toward Scotland's coastline. As I swam I opened and closed my hands to generate warmth. However, my skin had a white, almost greenish tone that scared me. The same thing was happening to my feet as if no blood flow was reaching my extremities. I knew the effects of cold water on the human body, so I wasn't surprised that this was happening, but when I saw it on my own body, I felt scared. I looked like a dead body! I kept repeating to myself a thousand times that I was fine, and at that precise moment, I got stung by another jellyfish. The sting and burn helped me generate the adrenaline in my body to keep on swimming.

I heard Nora yell out, "You are so close! Only about a kilometer and a half left to go." I realized that I would be in

Scotland soon and that this torture would be over.

Those last few meters in the jellyfish garden was bittersweet. I was leaving behind one less challenge to complete the Oceans Seven challenge and a year of preparation that seemed to have vanished into thin air. I didn't want this to end. I felt another sharp burn from what would be the last jellyfish in this journey and with the intense pain I let out my enthusiasm, happiness, and love for what I was about to accomplish. I felt a magnanimous gift being able to swim across the North Channel from Ireland to Scottland. When I finally reached the rocks, my heart was overwhelmed with gratitude and with much nostalgia for the adventure I was leaving behind.

Once I touched the rocks on the coast of Scotland, I heard the horn from the boat signaling that my swim was over and it had been validated. After swimming for thirteen hours and fifteen minutes, I realized that the jellyfish had helped me avoid hypothermia because with each sting and burn I was able to complete my swim of the North Channel.

Today, whenever I close my eyes and think back to that challenge, I can see the beautiful jellyfish floating in their garden in the Artic sea. I almost want to go back to touch and swim with them again, but perhaps this time only doing so in my mind. I can still feel the cold which I have decided to remember as love not only for the North Channel but also for each day of my life and any swimming challenge I will continue to undertake.

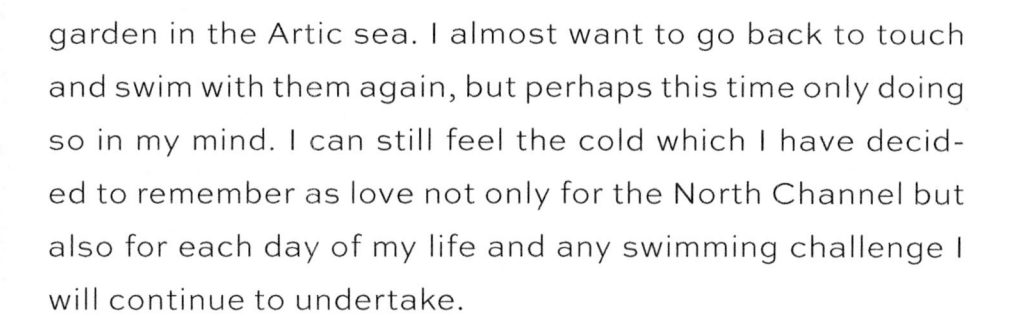

"The trip began a long time ago, almost 3,000 days. About eight years ago, even longer, I can't recall. I cannot keep track of time in the ocean, at least not by conventional means set up by humanity.

What I do clearly know is, that day will remain in my memories and on my body, marked by seawater, stars and the ocean, but above all with the certainty that I will never be left adrift because my seed was sown in heaven!"

Cook's Strait, New Zealand, March 2019.

CHAPTER 13
THE COOK STRAIT

By the end of July 2020, it seemed that a new normality was coming back into our daily lives, with new rules and an uncertain future, but at the same time, giving us a respite to continue moving forward. International news talked about a COVID-19 vaccine that was in trial stages and would be available in the coming months.

We learned to take care of ourselves to avoid infection- to leave the house only when absolutely necessary and to look for a few minutes of fresh air to enjoy the sun or to take a stroll during sunset.

Some of us were able to enjoy confinement: being able to share time with family and appreciate, like never before, that we were all healthy. But for others, this was not the case. Once the initial wave of fear subsided and while quarantine regulations were still in effect, the rate of domestic violence increased significantly as did the lack of attention for the elderly. Both of these circumstances experienced an increase in deaths and was putting many others at risk.

Every night I would watch the news from different media. I wanted to find out if the vaccine was finally ready or if any other medications were available. I learned that New Zealand had closed its borders and very few people got the virus. Apparently, all of these months of confinement hadn't been as necessary over there and the adequate sanitary measures needed hadn't been implemented either. I was so impressed with this bit of news that I found myself thinking back to my crossing of Cook's Strait.

On March 24th, 2019, when the plane landed in Wellington, New Zealand, after more than twenty hours of traveling from Mexico City and layovers in Los Angeles and Auckland, I thought, "I am about to complete the Oceans Seven Challenge and the only swim I need to complete is the Cook Strait."

What I didn't consider at that moment was that first, I needed to complete the swim! That's life…sometimes we think that we are only a step away from achieving something, and all of a sudden, when we are actually in the process of that final step, we realize that things get complicated and it isn't as easy as we had originally thought.

On March 30th, the alarm clock sounded at two in the morning and while somewhat still sleepy I thought, "Only the Cook Strait swim and I'll be done! I will have completed the Oceans Seven challenge." As if it were that simple! I woke up and got ready to get to the Wellington Marine on time at 4 am. I was excited and happy. Feeling rushed, I didn't have a lot to eat for breakfast, only a banana, a couple of cookies, and some coffee.

At the Marina we had to wait a few hours until the process to prepare the boats was completed. Three of us would be swimming in this challenge: Liz Fry, Nora Toledano, and myself. During previous months, Nora and I discussed completing Oceans Seven together, which is how we had planned. It seemed like an incredible way to finish a project we had shared for many years. However, once in Wellington, Nora told me she would swim with Liz Fry in tandem and I would swim with another boat and crew. I was sad when I heard this, but I supposed it was because of our swimming pace or speed, and anyway, we would both be completing the challenge the same day.

Gela was part of my support team and would be aboard the Zodiac during the entire swim. Lalo Perez, a good friend,

Olympic Swimmer, bronze medal winner in the Panamerican Games, who also played in many famous rock and roll bands, had also joined this adventure and would be in the guide boat supporting Gela in the preparation of all the supplies and taking photos and shooting videos, among other responsibilities.

Preparing everything for the swim, meeting with the crew at the Marina, and navigating to the starting point took a few hours. It was getting close to nine in the morning when I finally jumped in the water. I swam well for the first two or three hours. I was flying through the water, feeling like a dolphin myself. However, I started feeling hungry, and that became my first problem.

I would stop every half an hour to get my hydration drink full of protein and carbs. At one point, however, I became so hungry that I wanted something solid and delicious like a chocolate cake, chicken tacos, a hotdog, or a sandwich, not a bland hydration drink. Gela gave me a couple of crackers and a small bite of sandwich that the captain had taken with him aboard the Zodiac.

A few hours later, I began to feel a sharp pain in my lower

abdomen. "This can't be happening to me!" I thought. This was the second problem. I kept on swimming, but after a few minutes, I asked for help. "Please, I need something for the pain." At the next stop, Gela gave me a painkiller. I only needed to wait for the medication to start working so that I could continue swimming with no pain.

Five hours into the swim, my watch stopped working and I was no longer able to track time. The sun was still out in the blue sky, and the wind began to blow, and the surf made swimming more difficult.

I thought about that morning when I said to myself, "Only Cook is left..." and understood that things would not be so easy.

I had lost track of how long I had been swimming and had the feeling that the sun would be setting soon. I began to feel the waters' temperature as cool and even though the temperature wasn't bothering me, I did feel the cold in my hands and my fingers were getting numb. I thought I had been swimming for about nine hours at that point.

I didn't know how much time was left to reach the coast. I

focused on swimming and feeling energized so that I could beat the current which was making it difficult to reach the South Island of New Zealand.

Being able to swim Cook Strait was the final part of a lifetime project that I started more than eight years ago, back in 2011 when I crossed the English Channel. This was the final challenge to complete Oceans Seven, which consisted of swimming seven long-distance swims. Specifically, the English Channel, the Catalina Canal, the Strait of Gibraltar, the Molokai Channel, the Tsugaru Strait, the North Channel, and finally, Cook Strait.

As I kept swimming, I thought back to everything this endeavor had meant to me, and I went back to many memories of my life.

I remember the first time I held a baby in my arms that had been born with cleft lip and palate (CLP). It had made a strong impact on me. I could barely look at him because of his deformity. The pain I felt was not only for him but also for his mother who was barely sixteen years old and didn't know how to handle this little baby that couldn't suck to feed and wouldn't stop crying. That day, my dad asked me to go with him to the hospital because he had a consultation with a patient who was born with this deformity. I realized at that moment that I could help these families. And so, I did. For many years, I swam to raise funds for many surgeries for the benefit of low-income Mexican children who suffered from cleft lip and palate, inviting different organizations to donate funds for each kilometer swum.

On this journey, I was met with the generosity of Alejandro Marti and the Alfredo Harp Helu, A.C. Foundation. A few years later, swimming the English Channel, I couldn't stop thinking of my dad, who had passed away a few months prior, and I felt his love and presence that said to me, "Don't give up and finish what you started so that there can be many beneficial surgeries." And so, I did: I kept on swimming until completing the English Channel swim and helped transform the lives of many babies with this ailment.

The following year, in 2012, I swam the Catalina Channel and raised enough money to fund one hundred surgeries for children born with CLP. I was able to secure the generosity of the Alfredo Harp Helu, A.C. Foundation again. As I thought back to that moment, I smiled while I kept swimming.

I thought back to August 18th, 2013, as I swam from Battery Park, Manhattan, to Sandy Hook, New Jersey, a swim of twenty-five kilometers. It was an event in honor of Gertrude Ederle, an emblematic and visionary swimmer who was the first woman to cross the English Channel in 1926. Only five men had been able to complete this challenge before her and she had done so in record time. This woman has been my inspiration. After completing the English Channel swim, she returned to her hometown in New York to a parade in her honor where more than a million people participated. A short time later, Gertrude went deaf. She died at 97, alone. When I swam in Manhattan, I supported children with hearing loss problems through the Mexican Institute of Hearing and Speech Problems.

I thought of the deep look of two huge black eyes full of stars and the open smile of an eight-year-old boy whose thin body as a consequence of cancer didn't lose hope and demonstrated his faith. That look became the medicine for my sad and lonely soul caused by Eduardo's death due to the same illness. I also recalled the pain and sadness in Lalo and Andrea's faces as a result of their father's untimely death. My goggles filled with tears making me stop to empty them before I could continue swimming. I thought of the light in their eyes when they joined me in the swim in the Strait of Gibraltar. Gibraltar marked our lives- we left our sorrows in the ocean and completed the journey with the certainty that life goes on, and we must keep on swimming. I thought of Acapulco and Gibraltar; both swims in support of children with cancer through the Friendship House for Children with Cancer in Mexico City.

I kept on swimming as I recalled the storm at sea in the Tsugaru Strait, not only the physical surf, wind, clouds, and rain, but also my interior turmoil of anger, frustration, and anguish, to be met at the end with an inner calm that originated from the heart of that ocean. I went back to the end of that swim and how, when I got back on the boat, my only thought was, "I want a heart so full like the heart of the ocean…always in peace!"

I thought about the beauty of Hawaii and that sunrise swimming in the Pacific, with a silver moon hiding behind the horizon while the rays of the sun peeked in from the other side. I will never forget Nora's scream when she yelled, "Mariel, shark!" and the terrible fright we felt from that shark's visit.

I remembered my first visit to the Ecatepec Penitentiary, through the support of La Cana, a Mexican Association that helps women in prisons, in March 2018, to celebrate International Women's Day and be able to share my latest book "Días Azules" with the female inmates. I couldn't help but notice their looks of lost hope and how different the blue skies seemed from inside those prison walls. It made me realize how amazing the blue skies of freedom are. I decided to support this institution that helps with the rehabilitation of women who seek a second chance, not very different from me or you searching for new opportunities each day to make our dreams come true.

I heard Gela yell out from aboard the Zodiac and tell me that I needed to swim faster and stronger to counter the current that had taken me off course.

I thought back to my return to Japan with Andrea to complete a victory swim, and these memories filled me with hope with the intention I had set forth for myself then in the Tsugaru Channel: "Life always gives us another chance." In the middle of Cook Strait, that opportunity was coming to fruition.

Back in the North Channel, I had been immersed in the cold and in the midst of the jellyfish, but here, I hadn't seen even one, and it wasn't like I missed them, but I recognized that these beautiful but painful creatures had definitely helped me complete that difficult challenge.

As I kept swimming Cook Strait, I noticed that the ocean had turned pink, just as the sky did. The sun now behind the horizon. I was told that I had been swimming for about eleven hours and had only a few kilometers left. This ocean had been delicate and rough, even in good conditions... very rough! It had taken me a long time to override the currents to the point where I thought I wouldn't make it. Feeling at some point that I wasn't making any progress at all.

I wondered how Nora and Liz were doing. Were they close to finishing? Up ahead, I saw a boat come closer and both Liz and Nora were on it. They had completed the swim and were getting closer to cheer me on. They were celebrating! I felt sad when I thought that Nora and I would not complete the Seven Oceans together.

Swimming in that rosy sunset didn't last long; soon, night was upon me. In what seemed like an instant, I was surrounded by darkness, and I kept swimming without knowing how much more I had to go. I was feeling hungry and cold.

I intended to swim Cook Strait with the flow and feel part of the majestic ocean, but at that moment, I felt small, insignificant—a tiny dot in the middle of the ocean. I couldn't see the bubbles underwater nor the coastline that was supposedly close by. I was a tiny particle in the vast ocean and remember thinking. "Much more ocean and much less of me," and I said, "That is what I am doing, being much less of me and much more of the ocean."

I kept swimming in the darkness and stopped to try and see where the coast was. I knew I shouldn't waste time, but I needed to find the coastline to triple my efforts and complete this swim. When I stopped, Captain Philip Rush, aboard the Zodiac, couldn't see the blinking light I had on my cap because when I stopped suddenly, I was facing the boat and it was so dark that he couldn't see my silhouette in the water. He sounded the alarm and I heard his voice on the radio, "Mariel is adrift!"

The current had begun drifting me away. With each passing minute, my arrival at the coast was getting more complicated. The fact that they lost sight of me was also a sign of danger. When I heard his signal on the radio, I yelled at the top of my lungs, "I am here!" He said assertively, "Keep swimming and don't stop until you get there!" I knew at that instant that I wasn't adrift; I was simply much less Mariel and much more ocean, and it was what I needed to feel like part of the majestic vastness of the ocean and be able to complete this challenge.

My eyes filled with tears in this intimate moment as I kept swimming knowing that my yell, "I am here!" was an affirmation and certainty that I felt whole and complete, knowing where I stood, not feeling lost nor adrift, but in fact, on planet Earth, a tiny particle of ocean, between North Island and the South Island of New Zealand, swimming my final meters in Cook Strait, feeling much less me, but much more ocean, and making my dreams come true. Being more ocean, I kept on swimming until my hands felt something. I lifted my head up and could see rocks covered in moss, realizing at that moment that I had made it: "Being much less me and much more ocean." I held on to a rock and heard the horn signal from the boat. The swim was valid! My goggles were full of tears. I let go of the rock and fell into the water, floating on my back. I removed my goggles, and at that moment, I understood why I was there. My eyes were filled with thousands of stars that shone on me with their brilliant light, and I remembered someone telling me, "You will never be adrift because your seed was sown in heaven!"

I remained there floating as I looked up to the starriest sky that I had ever seen, my heart filled with so much gratitude. It took me eleven hours and forty-five minutes to swim Cook's Strait. I took a deep breath and swam to the Zodiac, which would take me to the escort boat that was about 300 meters away. When we got closer, I saw Gela waiting for me. She was crying, and as soon as I boarded the boat, she gave me a giant hug. As she held on to me, and I trembled, I heard her words: she congratulated me for my effort, commitment, and dedication of so many years to get to this moment. Lalo, overcome with what I had achieved, also hugged me and congratulated me.

I didn't celebrate with Nora as I had planned. She had already been celebrating for a few hours on her own. On our way back to Wellington, I thought of so many things, so many moments; some sad and others happy--but almost all of them magical. After so many hours in the water training and swimming thousands of kilometers to get to this moment, I felt incredibly proud of my journey that brought me here. The certainty that I always did it to support others, such as surgeries for children with cleft lip and palate, medical treatments for children with cancer, and support of women prisoners on their way back to society, among others. Also, in support, in one way or another, of those who had crossed my path during this journey. I felt a sense of accomplishment that I had company during this process and, in turn, I accompanied others in their personal journey. I understood deeply that I had been able to do all of it by being less me and much more ocean, and in that moment, I celebrated by myself, crying and smiling shedding my tears.

In March 2019, I became the sixth woman and the fifteenth person in the world to complete the Oceans Seven challenge.

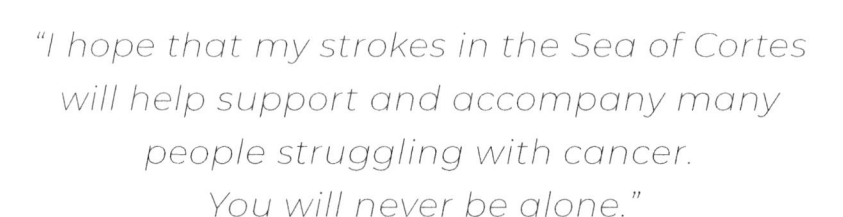

*"I hope that my strokes in the Sea of Cortes
will help support and accompany many
people struggling with cancer.
You will never be alone."*

**San Jose del Cabo, Baja California,
October 2019.**

CHAPTER 14
NEW SWIMMING ROUTES

Aquarium Swim

After I completed Oceans Seven, I felt happy to have finished such an ambitious challenge that had taken almost eight years of my life. I wasn't sure if I would continue swimming, but I knew that I wanted to share my experiences at sea and celebrate with my kids, friends, and family.

I let a few months go by only to realize that I couldn't stop swimming. I knew that swimming was very important to me and it had always been an activity that I loved!

As I reflected on all my previous swims, I realized that my strokes had splashed much more than water, giving a special meaning to each challenge and giving me a strong sense of fulfillment.

I made my decision: "I will continue swimming for the rest of my life!" I shared my decision with family members and friends. Some asked me, "That's great, but what will your next challenge be?" I didn't have any firm plans at that time, so I merely answered, "New open water swims!" But they kept on asking for more details—"Which ones?" I had no idea which ones, but I knew that something would guide me just as when I swam the 22-kilometer challenge in El Reto in Acapulco. Which is a swim route I inaugurated many years ago.

One day, I think it was in June, I got a call from Diego Rivas, the Los Cabos Open Water Challenge organizer, who proposed a new route. He shared his idea and in an instant, without any doubt, I told him I would be the first person to swim and open the new 32-kilometer route from San Jose del Cabo to Cabo San Lucas. He had named this swim route "Aquarium" in honor of Jacques Cousteau, who named the Sea of Cortes the "the aquarium of the world."

As I hung up the phone, I was already fully invested in this project and very excited to swim this new route that brought a promise to swim many kilometers and enjoy much of the marine wildlife in one of the most beautiful oceans in the world. The route would begin in the Sea of Cortes and end in the Pacific Ocean.

I didn't have much time to train and I hadn't done much

swimming since Cook. It wasn't until I got Diego's call to swim "Aquarium" that I realized how important it was to return to the water as soon as possible. I was worried that I would not have enough time to prepare and even though I had a strong background because of the thousands of kilometers I had swum in previous years, I was worried about a few other things. For instance, last November I had turned fifty years old, which meant that my body would be undergoing some changes that might affect my trainings. I, myself, felt those changes in me. When I was between thirty and thirty-five years old, I used to run once a week ten kilometers in combination with swimming as part of my physical conditioning. However, at fifty years old, the 10K running distance would exhaust me and wear me down terribly. It was also difficult to work out in the gym to build muscle mass, so I would prefer to exercise using resistance bands.

All of these thoughts had me wondering what would happen in the next fifteen or twenty years. Would I be able to continue swimming such long distances? How would my body react to the strenuous training necessary to tackle the next open-water challenges? Would I be able to withstand the cold temperatures as before? Can I hold out for eight, ten, twelve, or more hours in the water? I also thought of the emotional aspects. As the years went by, would I be getting more sensitive? On some mornings, I would surprise myself crying and wondered if it had anything to do with my aging, hormones, circumstances, or what I had dreamed the night before. Other days, I would wake up feeling elated, full of energy, and with the need to do all the things I hadn't yet accomplished: climb Everest, go to Australia, start a new business, play the piano, and take art classes. Then, suddenly, these feelings would disappear and I would go on with my regular day and responsibilities. One of the most notable changes was my hunger. I was hungry all day long and would crave sweet and chocolaty foods. I would ask myself, "Is this normal?" "Does this happen to other women my age?" "Are these the changes my doctor mentioned?"

The ocean tides change periodically, and I decided that my life's tides would, too, so I would just let things flow.

I decided to keep swimming and continue enjoying myself. I wanted to continue living the way I like and enjoy nature, the ocean, the sunrises, and every moment I was alive. With these thoughts in mind, I took a hold of the "Aquarium" project in earnest.

On Saturday, October 19th, 2019, at three thirty in the morning, we got together at the starting point of "Aquarium." Before I began this adventure, I took a moment to thank my support crew and shared a brief reflection of what this swim meant to me: on one hand, it was an opportunity to open up a new route in the wonderful Sea of Cortes, on the anniversary of Eduardo's birthday, as a way to celebrate his life along with Lalo and Andrea. Another important reason for this swim was to raise awareness about early detection of breast cancer. As a family, we learned that cancer has to be faced straight on and with a lot of courage—not only by the person suffering the illness but also by loved ones who will be supporting him or her throughout the treatment and fight against cancer. I told my crew, "I hope that with each stroke swimming in the Sea of Cortes we will aid and support many people struggling with cancer; whoever they may be, they are not alone." As a sign of my gratitude and humility, I offered a beautiful desert flower to the open sea, hoping it would allow me to begin my swim.

Gela, Vero—a dear childhood friend of mine—and Hector—the captain aboard the escort boat—along with his crew. Diego, the organizer of the challenge, and Rene, an excellent kayaker, would take turns on the kayak during the entire journey. I began swimming at 3:48 am enjoying the dark sea and the starry sky. At dawn I began to feel the pressure of the current coming from the Pacific Ocean, which made my swim somewhat difficult. Despite this, I kept up my rhythm. I swam for a few hours and watched thousands of colorful fish passing me by on my way to Punta Ballena. At that point, the current from the Pacific was too strong and wasn't allowing me to reach the bay at Cabo San Lucas; although I was swimming as hard as I could, I wasn't making any progress. I was beginning to lose my patience.

One of the worst things that can happen while you swim, or in life in general, is to despair. Sometimes, a momentary difficulty or uncertainty, a hopeless effort, or a combination of all of these situations causes you to try and find a quick way out, and you despair. That was where I was as I tried to reach Cabo San Lucas and I had already been swimming more than eight hours. I wasn't making any progress and I was completely desperate!

I thought back to when I participated in Swim Across the Sound on August 5th, 2017. The event was a twenty-five kilometer marathon from Port Jefferson to Bridgeport,

Connecticut. The challenge involved swimming across Long Island Sound. This event has been organized every year over thirty years ago in support of the cancer center at St. Vincent Hospital, which attends low-income patients from the area. I recalled that when I was on the ferry on my way from Bridgeport to Port Jefferson at five thirty that morning it started to rain and the rain turned into a storm.

The storm passed quickly, and the event was moved back an hour despite strong winds and light rain. When I jumped in the water, I remembered thinking, "Another storm in my life..." and began swimming.

As I crossed the Long Island Sound, many boats passed me by even though I was swimming with all my might. I felt like I wasn't moving forward, much less passing any of them. My feeding stops were fast, never exceeding thirty or forty seconds. After eight hours in the water, as much as I tried to push forward, the current wouldn't allow me to make any progress—I was stuck in the same place no matter how hard I tried to move forward.

I never stopped swimming knowing that I was rapidly approaching the ten-hour time limit for this swim. I asked the captain, Kevin Blanco, to allow me to continue swimming even after the time limit was over. I wanted to complete the challenge for myself even if it wouldn't be a valid swim. Kevin answered, "Keep swimming, and we'll see what happens." And that's what I did. I made it into the marina almost eleven hours after I jumped in the water. My emotions were all over the place. I felt proud that I had completed the event but I also felt frustrated that I was not able to complete the swim in the allotted time. I felt sad that my effort wouldn't count as a valid swim but, above all, I was very proud that I did not despair and that I never gave up swimming until I reached the finish line.

As I swam the last few meters, I thought, "Mariel, be very proud; you finished. Even if there isn't anyone waiting at the docks, you never gave up!"

A few minutes later, I reached the staircase at the dock, and I held on with both hands. I climbed three steps to get out of the water and heard cheers and yells from the crowd. Once out of the water and with my goggles still on, I received the most special welcome ever after completing a swim.

The applause lasted for a few seconds, and my eyes filled with tears of happiness and gratitude." I smiled as Liz Fry, the director of the event, came closer to give me a hug. She said, "We were all waiting for you because 'hope has no end' nor a definite term of completion!"

That day, my swim was one of hope to support the people who were fighting cancer. Once on the dock, I was told that the boats that had passed me by carried swimmers who had given up and were coming back to port. I never gave up!

The following day, at the awards ceremony, there was a religious ecumenical service in memory of those battling cancer. There were hundreds of flowers, each flower representing a victim who is still part of our lives only in our memory. As the flowers floated away, bagpipes sounded with a deep, melancholy melody that touched us deeply in our souls.

There are moments when words aren't enough to express what one is feeling and this was one of those very special moments. I will never forget the flowers floating in the tide and the bagpipes' melody sounding in the distance.

Watching those flowers floating towards the horizon, I thought about how life is never over; it is only transformed.

Thinking back to those moments, I kept on swimming in the Sea of Cortes. I moved past my despair and kept going until I finally saw the beautiful rock arc of Cabo San Lucas. I still had about 4 kilometers to go, but on that last part of the swim, I had my children's company! Lalo, Andrea, my mom, my aunt Alejandra, and Miguel, Gela's husband, met us on a boat to come with me on the last few kilometers. Andrea, my daughter, swam beside me while Lalo kept cheering us on from the boat.

I enjoyed those last few meters as I reached Medano Beach at 2:02 pm and was able to inaugurate the Aquarium swim from San Jose del Cabo to Cabo San Lucas in ten hours and fourteen minutes!

"The tide has changed... I breathe lightly and smile, and my eyes reflect the stars. My body feels it, as it is covered with shells of many shapes and colors.

The deep ocean is filled with life, like my thoughts that travel the universe, and the darkness of the ocean floor is illuminated with a bright light, as it is reflected in what my eyes can see."

Bahía de Banderas, October 2020.

CHAPTER 15
THE CORAZÓN DE MAR— BANDERAS BAY SWIM

The lockdown forced us to remain isolated and in doing so, several deep rooted emotions surfaced. I felt an innate need to hug my mom and my children, spend time with them, and keeping them close. I needed to spend time with my sister and her children, be close to my nephews, and watch them grow. I felt a small window of my heart open up that had been shut off for very long. I was feeling lonely and considered the possibility of opening my heart. However, it seemed challenging to meet someone in the midst of the pandemic, so I discarded those thoughts. I did start thinking of a new challenge, though, and a new project was born: Bahia de Banderas, a new swim!

At the end of August 2020, once the authorities opened up travel to beaches and national tourist centers, I traveled to Puerto Vallarta to start this new project, another new swim route. I was impressed by the distance between Punta de Mita and Cape Chimo, which was 34 kilometers long. Longer than the distance between Dover and Cap Gris-Nez in the English Channel! I loved the idea of crossing the beautiful Bahia de Banderas while swimming and took advantage of the trip to begin training. I went from one point to the other by boat, swimming short distances as part of my training.

I remember my childhood by the sea. The best vacations were spent in Acapulco. There wasn't anything better than spending entire days in my swimsuit and in the water. Many of these trips were shared with my sister, Aline, and our maternal grandparents. They would wake up early in the morning and take long walks on the beach. We would join them and, as we walked, grandmother would pick sea shells that piled up on the beach right next to the dry sand. My favorite shells were called "butterflies" because they were two halves stuck together. They were usually purple or pink and they looked like tiny butterfly wings when you opened them. I remember one time when we reached the other end of the beach; I told my grandmother that I was too tired to continue walking on the beach. I had burned the soles of my feet the day before because I walked on the hot sand at midday when the sun was at its peak. In addition to the burn on the soles of my feet, I also had a small cut on my heel that would hurt every time I took a step. The idea of having to walk back was a torturous one.

"Grandma, please let me go back swimming... I beg you!" I said.

Grandpa looked at me incredulously and said, "Honey, are you crazy? Do you think a nine-year-old young girl can swim that far?"

I answered immediately, "Of course I can Grandpa! You'll see that I can do it!" I assured him and without thinking twice about it I ran to the water and jumped in. My feet felt wonderfully relieved. The seawater had a healing effect helping me with the pain and burning sensations on my feet. I began swimming back to where we were staying while my grandparents and sister walked along the beach. I was swimming breaststroke keeping my head above water and as close to the waves as possible. Whenever I felt my feet touch the sand, I would swim back out to a place where the water was deeper. As I kept swimming along, the waves were getting bigger and come down even harder on me. I learned to be on the other side of the wave so that it wouldn't toss me around. It required a bit more effort to swim but I was able to see my grandparents watching me and walking slowly as they waited for me. I swam a few strokes of crawl and opened my eyes while swimming. At that moment, I discovered that if I kept my eyes opened while my head was underwater, I could see everything and that my eyes didn't sting as much as they did when a small drop of salt water got into my eyes! I also discovered that if you swim behind the wake it doesn't toss you around! I made all of these discoveries while my grandparents and sister walked along. I enjoyed what became my first actual swim in open waters. I felt a sense of joy and, above all, I felt free and had fun!

As I got out of the water, grandpa was waiting for me and with a look of wonder on his face, he said, "Honey, you are probably going to get fish scales; not even mermaids swim that much!" I really didn't know how to respond to his words so I simply laughed. Grandpa asked if I was okay. "Of course. I am so happy!" I exclaimed. That was one of the most magical moments of my life.

During my training in Bahia de Banderas, I enjoyed the ocean just as I did when I was a little girl. I always had company; playful and curious dolphins would swim by my side. I got to know the Marieta Islands, the church zones, the small town of Chimo, and I loved swimming in one of the largest bays in the world, all of which was in the most beautiful sea, the Pacific Ocean.

The pandemic also allowed for new ways to communicate, bringing an unexpected surprise into my life. Through a Zoom meeting, I met Gerardo! A group of friends from Club Reforma had invited me to reconnect online so that we could catch up and chat. I decided to join the meeting as a way to have some "social life."

I wanted to touch base to see how everyone was doing and if they were doing well. Someone asked me, "And you, Mariel, are you still swimming?" I went on to tell them about my plan to swim the Bahia de Banderas, and when Gerardo heard me, he told me I was completely crazy! I just laughed! Everyone seemed interested in my new project, and I was happy to tell them all about it.

The swim in Bahia de Banderas was getting closer, and I was getting more and more excited. I had been preparing everything for the trip until finally, the day arrived. My children, Lalo and Andrea, would come on the trip, just as would my friends Gela and Vero, who would be my support crew. The swim was scheduled to start at six in the afternoon at Cape Punta de Mita and would take all night long to swim approximately 34 kilometers to reach Chimo—a tiny fishing village in the southernmost part of Bahia de Banderas.

On October 23rd, at 7:05 pm, I hugged my children on the boat, giving them all of my love and as we held on to each other I thanked God for their lives and for the majestic and imposing ocean that awaited me to swim in it during the next few hours until morning the next day. After kissing Lalo and Andrea I jumped in the water to begin swimming across Bahia de Banderas.

The sunset was beautiful as seen from the water. I could see the red ball hiding behind the clouds as it colored them in orange and pink hues. While my strokes painted the water with bubbles that left a wake behind me, the horizon turned red and the sun began to hide behind the ocean little by little. When I finally saw the last ray of sun light, it seemed like the sun was sinking into the water and my heart jumped out of my chest. I felt as if my heart had skipped a beat when I thought about Gerardo and what he said when we said goodbye a few days ago: "I will be thinking about you all the time!"

Before I knew it, night fell, and everything got dark and silent. The ocean's surface had a mysterious shine and I could feel a light breeze on my back. It was so dark that I couldn't see the horizon and could barely see the small light on the boat up ahead.

After about four hours, I began feeling a loneliness that I had only felt when swimming in the ocean at night. It is like being in a separate and distant place, where you can only hear the winds and the sound of the water. It is like swimming in a dark liquid and, in this moment without any bioluminescent glow of marine life, the ocean seemed a dark and gloomy place.

I thought of my children, my mom, and the girls from the orphanage Corazon de Niña, "Girl's Heart", that I had visited a few months ago. Right after my visit, I decided that the Bahia de Banderas swim would support this organization. A few days before the actual swim, some of the girls came to visit me at the hotel and after spending time together they told me they would be praying for my safety. I thanked them and hugged them. I felt moved while I swam and remembered those moments, knowing that they would be with me and praying for me at a distance. I was filled with a sense of peace. Despite their suffering and lack of resources, these girls had enormous faith and love which they shared with me during those hours at night. I kept on swimming as I held on to those positive thoughts, trying to enjoy myself with each stroke I took.

When I stopped after six hours of swimming to get my hydration drink, Gela told me we were doing well, on route, and we were more than halfway there. Vero told me that Gerardo had called to tell me he was thinking of me and would be with me during the entire journey. I felt excited at hearing his message, and my heart swelled with joy. Happy and excited I continued swimming and a few minutes later the dolphins appeared! I couldn't see them, but I could hear them and felt them nearby. They kept me company all the way to Chimo during the last three hours it took me to get there. They would swim close and then move further away. I am not certain they were the same ones or others who would join me, but I know that, even though it was a long swim and the night was dark, I never lacked company. Vero and Gela were caring for me from the boat. I also felt the presence of Gerardo and the girls from the orphanage Corazon de Niña. After nine hours and fourteen minutes, at around four in the morning, tired but very happy, I got out of the water in Chimo.

That afternoon, I celebrated my crossing of the Bahia de Banderas in a special way with the girls from Corazon de Niña.

Once back in Mexico City, I became aware that the tides had turned for the better. The tides of my life changed, just like they do in the ocean when they rise and fall, generating marine currents and other vital phenomena for our planet. My personal tides also transformed, instilling new emotions that filled me with energy and vitality.

Gerardo came into my life, and the tides had changed for me. I began to breathe lighter and smile more, and there was a special light reflected in my eyes. My body felt it too and the depth of my emotions filled with life, just as my thoughts traveled across the universe. The darkness of my ocean filled me; its intense brightness mirrored back in Gerardo's eyes. I celebrated my success in the Bahia de Banderas alongside with him, and that is how a new tide of my life began for me, with a happy, fun love, full of new adventures and new journeys to swim.

CHAPTER 16
THE COZUMEL — PUNTA MAROMA SWIM

Christmas 2020 was utterly different from the others before. When fall began in Mexico City, the number of COVID-19 cases was on the rise and many people who had returned to their regular routines caught the virus. Plans to spend the holidays together were canceled and Christmas parties, family reunions, and get-togethers with older relatives would not be possible since they were at a high risk of catching the virus.

In my case, December 24th was special because it was Gerardo's birthday along with the Christmas celebration. For the first time our two families had dinner together. One could say that the pandemic brought our families together. I am sure that the same was true for many other families worldwide.

In January 2021, reality came crashing down. There were many cases of COVID-19 and there was much fear of catching the virus. Deaths were rampant because patients didn't receive the necessary care and there was a sense of uncertainty regarding all aspects of life as we once knew. The good news was that the vaccines were in trial stages; the bad news was that we didn't know how or when we would be able to get the vaccines in Mexico. But the worst news of all reached me by way of a telephone call.

During mid-January, my mother went to Acapulco for a few days to escape the cold temperatures in Mexico City knowing that she would have to self-quarantine while she was there. I called her one day and when she answered the phone she seemed disoriented; her voice was weak and her words didn't make any sense. She told me she was exhausted and couldn't walk. Without giving it a second thought, I immediately jumped in the car and drove to Acapulco. I spoke to her doctor and he gave me two dire possible causes: a brain stroke or COVID. As soon as I saw her, my heart stopped. She wasn't herself. She couldn't talk, was half asleep, her words did not make any sense at all, and she couldn't stand up either. The hospitals in Acapulco, private and public, were past their capacity due to the many COVID cases and emergency rooms didn't have sufficient resources for the number of people they had to treat. The doctor asked me to bring her back to Mexico City in the hopes of getting better medical attention. I tried to keep myself fully focused while I was driving back to Mexico City, but I couldn't help notice how my mother would babble incomprehensible words. My thoughts thinking the worst possible scenario for her. The doctor was waiting for us at the ER and ordered some tests as soon as we got there. Six hours later, we finally got the results back: positive for COVID-19. They would not let me see her or let me go into the hospital; I had no way of communicating with her and along with my kids, my sister, my aunt Ale, and I, we went through one of the worst moments in our lives. I was also at risk of infection because I had been with her in close proximity and closed space and it was required of me to be tested on a daily basis. Thankfully, all my COVID tests came back negative. After eight days of mother being in the hospital, I got a call from her doctor. I was so scared; I didn't want to answer the phone!

"Hi, doctor," my words came out quickly, laced with fear. "Mariel, your mother is a warrior. She survived COVID, and today we will be releasing her." I don't remember what else he told me because I started jumping up and down of joy. There aren't any words to describe the scene when mom was released from the hospital. She left in the midst of cheers and applause from the nursing staff and they accompanied her all the way to the hospital's exit. When I saw her coming out in a wheelchair, I couldn't stop shedding tears. My face mask hid my smile, but it couldn't hide or contain the tears of joy I felt at that moment. I wasn't supposed to get close to her, but I couldn't help myself and gave her a giant hug. She got up from her chair, and I ran to her and held her tightly. To this day, she is still recuperating (March 2023). She got the vaccine and booster but was infected by the virus again after a year from her first bout of COVID-19.

Later that same year, the Hard Rock Riviera Maya Hotel invited me to a conference in June 2021. They wanted to reactivate certain activities and invite speakers for the staff and clients. I decided it would be a good idea to swim the Cozumel-Mayan Riviera and invited Gerardo on this adventure. I ran the idea by him and he was excited to be a part of my support team, so we began planning the project in earnest.

On June 10th, 2021, a few minutes before six in the morning, I hugged Gerardo on the boat, gave him a kiss, and jumped in the water on my way to the beach at Hotel Presidente in Cozumel. That was the starting point of my swim towards the Mayan Riviera. Onboard the boat was Myrza Ortega, a Playa del Carmen swimmer, acting as judge, along with Alonso Ramirez, a fellow swimmer, and Captain Rodrigo Torres and his assistant Diego Ponce de Leon.

I had spent a few minutes on the beach, and when the horn sounded at the start of the swim at 6:06 am, I began the journey. The sea was turquoise. Like a mirror it reflected the pink clouds in the sky. I swam, enjoying Gerardo's presence on the boat. I could see him enjoying himself, happy, and participating in everything that was going on—keeping count of my strokes per minute, my feeding stops, the route, and watching the dolphins that came to visit me. We had an early morning rain shower and a rainbow that pointed the way from Cozumel to the north of the Mayan Riviera. It was nature smiling on Gerardo and me for what we had started a few months earlier and what we were solidifying in these shared moments.

I swam from Hotel Presidente in Cozumel to Maroma Point in the Mayan Riviera for seven hours and twenty-three minutes. A dream of a swim! The celebration? Incredible! With music and lots of rock!

"I've always said it: I love swimming, and it fills me with life, but swimming in the ocean is magical!

The ocean calls me to a new adventure: to a new Viking route—the Oresund Strait! A swim between Denmark and Sweden."

Copenhagen, Denmark, August 2022.

CHAPTER 17
THE ORESUND SWIM

At the end of 2021, I got an email from someone called Dennis inviting me to swim the Strait of Oresund. After reading the message, I deleted it and forgot about it. Two weeks later, I got another email requesting my response to their invitation. At first, I thought it was part of a list of recipients and decided to check who had also received these messages to see if I knew anyone in the invite list. I was surprised to see that I was the only recipient. I responded by asking them to give me two weeks to think about it and I would get back to them. I thought it was a good way to gain some time and maybe Dennis would lose interest. But I kept thinking, What was Oresund? So, I looked it up on Google Maps and realized that it was the strait between Denmark and Sweden and I made a first quick decision: there was no way I would be going because I didn't want to do another cold water swim. I have done enough!

Two weeks later, I got a call from Dennis, and before I could say, "No thanks," he started explaining the importance of this swim and how strategic this strait has always been in history. I fell in love with the idea that Shakespeare had found his inspiration in Elsinore Castle, which was at the edge of the sea where he wrote Hamlet. I was also interested in knowing that the Vikings had sailed these waters in search of new distant lands.

After hanging up, I told Gerardo about my conversation with Dennis and went on to tell him what I had decided. I was going! Gerardo said, "Mariel, I would love to go with you!" Everything happened in a blink of an eye. The distance training, cold water temperatures, La Jolla, California, Las Estacas, the "Esmeralda" pool, and finally, a trip to Denmark!

Swimming in the "Esmeralda" pool is like swimming in a freezer. I recall someone who told me was training to swim the English Channel, shared with me that she was swimming in a pool without heating in the Esmeralda zone in Mexico City. When I told her I was looking for a place to get used to the cold waters she was happy to take me there and that is how I ended up swimming in that freezer.

However, the freezer never lacks warmth due to the care and support from the owners and staff, Marcela Huitron and her daughter. They cheered me on every day during my training and shared delicious chocolates that gave me much-needed energy, and their attention was like a warm hug to withstand the cold water.

The Viking route was a wonderful adventure in a spectacular sea, the Oresund Strait between the North Sea in Denmark and the Baltic Sea in Sweden. On August 9th, at four in the morning, I began swimming from Bellevue Beach in Denmark, and after 20 kilometers and 8:59 hours of swimming, I completed the first historical swim recorded in the Oresund Strait at Lundakrabukten, Sweden.

That is how the Oresund Strait route was officially inaugurated and it will forever remain in my memory as my Viking Swim!

As I write this in March 2023, I remember my trip to Argentina exactly three years ago, in March 2020. I went there to swim across the Rio de la Plata. I think back to the transformation we all went through all over the world because of COVID-19 pandemic. I close my eyes and hold a minute of silence in memory of those who lost their lives because of this illness. I think about those who got sick and felt their lives fading away with each breath taken, keeping up the fight to stay alive. Among those, my mother, who I already talked about, was hospitalized in the COVID unit for eight days and had to use supplemental oxygen for three months after her recovery. Even after two vaccines, she was infected again and to this day, she still struggles with the many secondary health issues caused by this disease. I think about the doctors, nurses, and other healthcare professionals who risked their lives to help others. I send each and everyone my support and admiration. I think about the vaccination process and every routine situation that forever changed and transformed our lives because of the COVID-19 pandemic.

This transformation also touched an intimate part of my life, specifically related to my swimsuits! There are women who love shoes, bags, or dresses, but I love swimsuits! It is my favorite garment, for it holds a very significant aspect of my life. I almost never leave home without one, whether in my bag, backpack, or suitcase. I also always have a set of caps and goggles. For the last twenty years, I have had more swimsuits than any other clothing article. I love them, but they aren't very durable! Because I swim every day, they are put to good use, but deteriorate quickly—the straps get loose, the colors fade, and the lycra stretches and loses its shape. So, I am forced to buy new ones constantly.

I like both one-piece swimsuits and bikinis. I will choose one or the other depending on where I am swimming. I love the different prints and colors and usually pick bright ones. I have categorized some of my suits with different names based on their uses, such as "Speed," "Merengue," "Flower Garden," "Resistance," and "Patience," among others. If the training session includes a series of speeds, I wear the one with that name. If I will be swimming for many hours, I will wear the one called "Resistance with Happiness," and so on. Almost all have a first and last name!

The different swimsuits I've used during the specific challenges have a special place in my life. The one I wore during the crossing of the English Channel knows my secrets, my heart, and my feelings. It knows the effort and perseverance it took, especially when my physical endurance was reaching its limit. That suit still has a special scent—the scent of victory. The one I wore in the Catalina Channel is called "Light." It was with me during the eight-hour swim in the dark, and witnessed the effort I made with my heart to cross the channel. The suit I wore when I swam the island of Manhattan is white and gray with pink graffiti, perfect for the place and occasion.

I have swimsuits I use in competitions and have worn them exclusively in matches that take place in pools, never in open waters. Each day, I choose the suit to wear and have my favorites. The ones that make me feel comfortable swimming freely. I imagine that women who love certain dresses feel the same. Their favorites make them feel great. The ones I choose whenever I swim in open waters have their own name and "age." During the past challenges, I have found that there is always one ready for me to wear on that special day—the day of the crossing. I have kept all my suits in two drawers: in one, I put all the suits that I have worn, and in the other, I put the suits that I am currently using. But what they all have in common are the blue and marine memories they carry, each with their own special story.

However, a few months ago, I decided that it was time to transform the suits I wasn't wearing anymore, so I took them out and gave them to Geo, a friend, and artist who, with her creativity, would surely create something special with them. I have probably swum between 18 - 20 thousand kilometers during the past twenty years. Adding them up, I realize that each suit has seen a very long aquatic voyage full of memories that will remain transformed into a special work of art made by Geo.

The only swimsuit I kept and didn't give away to Geo was the one I wore when I was named "Woman of the Year" by the World of Open Water Swimming Association in 2020.

Who knows what the next swim will bring? But I am sure that the tides of life will take me to new places and swim for many more kilometers. If it isn't Argentina, it will certainly be another place. What I know for sure is that I will continue to flow with the incoming tides of life.

"I will swim with you in spirit, so that my effort will encourage you to keep going, inspire you not to give up, motivate you to get up the day you stumble, and above all, motivate you to dream big and to make your dreams come true.."

Mexico City, June 2023.

EPILOGUE

It is said that the ocean tides have followed mathematical patterns since the beginning of time. The tide generates marine currents and climate change; it rises and falls with the moon; it provokes tidal waves that seem like mountains; and, in other moments, it brings pink sunsets over a silky and luminous surface. The dolphins and whales know their marine routes thanks to the tides, and coral reefs adorn their pathways. The stars in the sky reflect on the water's surface. That is how the new tide of my life has been; I have cried while being held, laughed in the company of others, and sung and danced with the moon as my witness and with the stars shining on me. My family grew, and with a kiss, I was lost in a sea of emotions until I found myself feeling loved and held until sunrise.

The tides also transformed my children's lives. They have become independent young adults who are forging their own paths. The pain feels different at a distance—it doesn't disappear, but its intensity is different. I also feel that the sadness transforms, and I can see this in both Lalo and Andrea. Each has been able to transform their pain and sadness into emotions that allow them to move on with their lives as they try to meet their goals and objectives. When I catch a glimpse of their hearts through their eyes, however, I can see flashes of sadness and a scar that tries to heal a little each day. I also see bright flashes of light in their eyes when they talk about their plans for the future. I see them mature and with each step they take it fills me with pride. I see them smile and even laugh. I realize they have learned to keep swimming through life and I see their heart like the heart of the sea, always at peace.

The tides sometimes push and sometimes pull, but they always transform. They move back and forth, allowing marine life to flow and they also help those who seek to be more ocean so as to enjoy its majestic essence and life itself. The tides manifest grandeur through the minuscule microorganisms that generate life and light within.

This book is a testimony to what the tide has generated in my life. It is a way to "save," in a matter of speaking, the ocean patterns as part of my life, currents and countercurrents, the storms, and, above all, the transformation and continuous flow.

The testimony of the tides in my life allow me to come back

to relive and remember them. I find this important because the mind is like an ocean of infinite waves and perpetual motion, but even in its greatness, it doesn't always remember its patterns and its own tides. When that moment comes in my life, Rising Tides will be here to help remember and allow me to relive each memory. In the meantime, I hope Rising Tides travels the world and reaches you, keeping you company through whatever you are doing in your life. I hope it inspires you to be less of yourself and more of the sky, stardust, light, and, in essence, more of that which makes you happy and allows you to reach for your dreams.

ACKNOWLEDGEMENTS

This book, Rising Tides is a declaration of gratitude and praise. For those who wonder what it means to be less Mariel and much more Sea, it is precisely less of my negative parts and much more of my intimate parts that have gotten me closer to God in every moment, connecting me spiritually and allowing me to live in eternal gratitude. Thank God for the tides of blessings as my heart overflows with thankfulness.

I thank you, reader. Thank you for making Rising Tides a part of your life. I am sure that reading this book will help you discover your own tides and inspire you to reconnect with your dreams. The beauty of dreams is that they romance us each day subtly and delicately; they call us to follow them and make them a reality. That is what happens on a daily basis in this path, as they leave their mark and transform us with the constant flow of tides, as they wrap us with their magic. I invite you to enjoy your own tide and become aware of its changing currents, flow, and ebb of water. To be aware of everything that generates life, from the most intimate and small to the grand and majestic, so that you may find your path and rediscover your dreams.

Let the tide become a constant, harmonious flow in your life and, thank you for being a part of the tides in my life.

I will never tire of thanking Lalo and Andrea throughout my life, with all my love and devotion, for being my motivation.

Thank you, Mom, for being my pillar of love and because your hugs always fill me with peace.

Dad, you are still here. Your love and smile inspire me to move forward.

Eduardo, thank you for everything we created together because you still live on intensely through Lalo and Andrea.

A special thanks to you, Gerardo, for becoming part of my flowing tide. It fills me with joy to be able to share this stage of my life with you. Let's continue flowing together! I love you!

Thank you, friends—all of you. As time passes by, it seems that the tides of our lives have moved us apart, but remember that the currents of life are circular and always come back full circle. There will be moments when we may seem far apart, but in a moment the tide turns and we will be together again, sharing our lives just like we have always done in the past.

Thanks to all who have been a part of the process of Rising Tides. Your support has made this book possible, and I am sure it will navigate the oceans of life.

To the ocean, my deepest gratitude.

AWARDS AND RECOGNITIONS

2023

"Her for She Award"

Women supporting women.

Awarded by Hershey's Mexico

Mexico City

2022

"The Oresund Swimmer of the Year Award"

For the inaugural swim across the Oresund and support to Swim Oresund.

Marathon Swim between Denmark and Sweden.

2020

"Woman of the Year"

Awarded by the "World of Open Water Swimming Association (WOWSA)

2018

Guinness World Record for the Tsugaru Strait Swim

2015

"Omecihuatl Medal"
Awarded by the "Instituto de Mujeres de Ciudad de México.
Woman's Institute, Mexico City

2013

"Mont Blanc Award"
Category – "Woman Who Leads the Way"
Mexico City

2012

"Honorary Award"
Awarded by the Mexican Sports Institute and the Mexican Woman's Institute.
Mexico City

2011

"Women Strengthening Women Award"
Awarded by the "Observatorio para la Mujer de América Latina, A.C."
Mexico City

2007

Guinness World Record for the Four-Way Relay Crossing of the English Channel.

The Dover Straits Award
English Channel Swim
For the Fastest CS&PF Standard Relay Crossing

2007

Sport City México's 1st Leg of the Four Way England to France is 8 hours and 18 minutes.

Mariel Hawley Dávila

OPEN-WATER SWIMMER, WRITER & SPEAKER

Mariel is a lawyer from Universidad Iberoamericana, Mexico City and has previously worked at Basham Abogados, Banco Santander and Grupo Martí. Since 2017, she has directed Queremos Mexicanos Activos, A. C., a non-profit organization aimed at promoting physical activity as an integral part of a healthy lifestyle.

More than 20 years ago, Mariel embarked on the adventure of open water swimming and in March 2019, she became the 15th person in the world to accomplish the Ocean Seven Challenge.

In parallel to her career as a lawyer and open water swimmer, Mariel founded the "Quiero Sonreír" project, through which she channeled some of her swims to benefit low income Mexican children with cleft lip and palate with surgeries. Since 2015, she has supported Casa de la Amistad para Niños con Cáncer, I.A.P. Likewise, she has been a swimmer with a cause to support different organizations such as La Cana, A.C., and Angelitos con Autismo, A.C., among others.

Through her work in Queremos Mexicanos Activos, she organizes the event "Nado por mi Corazón" (Swim for your Heart Mexico), which has become the most important aquatic physical activity event in Mexico, whose objective is to generate awareness about heart care and through which surgeries have been generated for children with heart disease.

Mariel is an Ambassador for Special Olympics Mexico, author of "Días Azules", "Corazón de Mar" and "Rising Tides". She is also a key role speaker and currently lives in Mexico City.

CONNECT WITH MARIEL!